A Lift for Living

Ralph W. Sockman

A
LIFT
FOR LIVING

New York   **ABINGDON PRESS**   *Nashville*

A LIFT FOR LIVING

Library of Congress Catalog Card Number: 56-13464

C

SET UP, PRINTED, AND BOUND BY THE
PARTHENON PRESS, AT NASHVILLE,
TENNESSEE, UNITED STATES OF AMERICA

TO

Z. E. S.

who has given me
"A Lift for Living"
through more years
than she likes to admit

PREFACE

❖❖❖❖❖❖❖❖❖❖❖❖❖❖❖❖❖

The brief messages in this little book have been garnered from long sowing. It is my hope that they may serve as seed thoughts to start enriching ideas growing in the minds of their readers.

Great living comes by growth. The human body grows until it reaches adult size. Then we diet to prevent its expansion. But our personalities cannot remain static and be healthy. The mind either grows or loses. These discussions are designed to keep us on the growing edge of life.

For some years I have syndicated "A Lift for Living" as a column in the public press. I wish to express my gratitude to the editors who have carried this column and to Mr. S. George Little of the General Features Corporation for making the syndication possible. Also, I am indebted to Mr. Thornton Fisher and to Miss Juliet Endly for their assistance in the selection of material from my radio sermons. Mrs. Helen Stanbury, Miss Beatrice Meylan, and Miss Marion Marcy have rendered invaluable secretarial service. Zellah Endly Sockman has given the inspiration (and correction!) which only a wife can give.

RALPH W. SOCKMAN

CONTENTS

❖❖❖❖❖❖❖❖❖❖❖❖❖❖

9

I

When Spirits Are Low

❖❖❖❖❖❖❖❖❖❖❖

THE GIFT WITHIN YOU

If someone were to say to you, "Rekindle the gift of God that is within you," what would you think he meant? Most likely you would ask yourself, "What special gift have I?"

Commonly, when we speak of gifts of God, we think of unusual native endowments, such as a glorious singing voice, an artistic touch, or a power of literary expression.

Not many of us, however, have these outstanding talents in such degree that we could be called gifted. Most of us are just ordinary run-of-the-mill individuals. Even in our family life we may have been overshadowed by some more brilliant brother or sister. In school we were not singled out for special distinction. Since leaving school we have made no name which gets featured or no fortune worth mentioning.

Of course, we can always think of some persons who seem less gifted than ourselves. Hence, when we feel dwarfed in the presence of our superiors, we can build up our egos by taking a look at those who seem less favored. But in the long run it is not too satisfying to depend on the apparent inadequacies of others for our own well-being.

Emerson once said, "Every man I meet is my superior

in some way. In that, I learn of him." What if we caught Emerson's insight and attitude, and instead of concerning ourselves with our own traits, we were to study the traits of others, looking for their gifts that we might learn of them and link ourselves with them? Certainly such an attitude would enrich our inner lives and sweeten our relationship with our fellow, men.

Before me is a letter written by an elderly man. The snows of age were upon him, but the light of his eyes was undimmed. He was like a house lighted up on a winter evening. Such houses make me think of some lives. The writer of this letter was in prison awaiting expected execution as a martyr, but his hardships had not put out the fire of his spirit.

He wrote to rckindle the enthusiasm of a young friend. So far as we know, this young man was not of exceptional ability. But he had something which is possessed by every one of us. That something is a spirit which the writer thus defines: "Rekindle the gift of God that is within you through the laying on of my hands; for God did not give us the spirit of timidity but a spirit of power and love and self-control." Such was the counsel which Paul wrote to young Timothy.

Let us consider one of these gifts of God. Take the spirit of power. Paul says, "Rekindle" it. And the word he uses suggests the stirring of a fire. When a fire has died down, what is the first thing we do to it? We poke it. That's what most of us need when we get into our low moods of fearfulness. We should immediately try to shake ourselves out of such unworthy states.

When the fires of faith and courage need reviving, we must bestir our wills to action. Then we must put more fuel into our minds. A good coach does not merely shout orders to his team; he builds up their morale as well.

Think how Jesus coached the apostles. Not only did he stir their wills, but he fed their minds with thoughts like these: "Fear not, little flock, for it is your Father's good pleasure to give you the kingdom"; or "I go to prepare a place for you." Such thoughts rekindle hope.

Years ago a friend of mine, a frail little woman, was being taken on a Mediterranean cruise to restore her health. Her husband died on the voyage. She came back to the difficult task of raising her ten children. She lost two of her four sons in World War I. Still her tireless energy and indomitable spirit amazed those who knew her. She simply abounded in good works.

What was the secret of her strength? It was this: she used her iron will to stir up God's gift within her and kept refueling her mind with her religious faith.

❖❖❖❖❖❖❖❖❖❖❖

MASTERING PAIN

There is no trait which evokes more admiration in our time than that of masterfulness. And there is no achievement of which we can more rightfully boast than our increasing mastery of the material things around us.

Truly it would seem that we are fulfilling the biblical promise of the Creator that man should have dominion over the earth. And now scientists are predicting travel to the moon within twenty-five years.

But with all our mastery of the movable factors around us, are we improving our self-mastery when we confront the immovable obstacles of life? Has our efficient age of science so accustomed us to getting things done by quick mechanical means that we are at a loss when all we can do is stand and take it?

Let us consider one of life's immovables, pain. Before we call pain one of life's immovables, we should recall how much pain has been removed through the healing art and scientific prevention. "The ills that flesh is heir to" were far more numerous in the days of Shakespeare than now. Man has learned to quiet nerves with sedatives, to make us oblivious of the surgeon's knife through anesthetics, to stop the ravages of disease.

And there are no doubt many new frontiers of advance in the prevention of pain. No longer should we blindly drift into disease and disaster, then piously call them the will of God.

When we neglect the principles of health and fall sick, or when we neglect efforts for peace and get into war, it is blasphemy to blame the suffering on God. God holds us responsible for using all our resources to ward off accident, disease, disaster, and death.

Nevertheless, in spite of our best efforts there is bound to be some pain of which we all get a share. Love, the most beautiful thing in life, carries in it the possibilities of intense pain, caused by anxiety, abuse, or death. Every extension of love and friendship enlarges our exposure to the possibilities of pain.

What help can we get from God in mastering irremovable pain?

Well, we can acquire a better sportsmanship in our attitude. Do we not have to admit that most of us make more commotion over little hurts than serious ones? How commonly we advertise our slight disorders which nobody sees and make light of the serious injuries.

Let a husband sprain his wrist while helping move

the piano, and repeatedly he calls his wife's attention to his discomfort! But let her come to visit him in the hospital where he lies after an almost fatal accident, and he quiets her outbursts of sympathy as if his injury were trivial.

Does not this attitude suggest that some of our attention to pain is due to our desire to seek the sympathy of others? Most of us must admit that we do not show very good sportsmanship in mastering our minor pains.

Another secret in the mastery of pain is the use of the imagination. Robert Louis Stevenson in 1893 wrote that for fourteen years he had not had one day of real health. Though racked with pain he wrote the books which boys still read, such as *Treasure Island*.

Even when he became so ill that his doctors forbade him to talk or write, he tried to dictate in sign language the conclusion of the book he was writing. He turned the stream of his thoughts into the bright, active world until his darkened room ceased to exist for him during long periods of time.

Also, God can transform our pain into power, as he did for Paul. Paul had a physical affliction which he prayed to have cured. God did not remove it, but he did say to Paul, "My grace is sufficient for you, for my power is made perfect in weakness." Having discovered this, Paul said: "I am content with weaknesses, insults, hardships, persecutions, and calamities; for when I am weak, then I am strong."

Pain and adversity may serve us as the headwind serves the pilot. The headwind may slow the plane's speed, but the pilot must head into it if he wants to get off the ground.

CONTROLLING THE BACKWARD LOOK

The art of leaving is a vital part of the art of living. A popular essayist tells of a certain clergyman who made such a success of his first pastorate that after seven years he was called to a larger parish. So firmly was he rooted in the love of his work that he declined the tempting invitation. Then his trouble began. From that time forth, whenever the least thing went wrong in his church, his thoughts turned toward his lost opportunity at the other place. Whenever the mood of depression overtook him, he dreamed of the declined offer.

He would have saved himself infinite mental distress if he could have cut off decisively the thought of "what might have been." Eight years later he did leave his parish for another. Then after the excitement of the new venture had subsided, the periods of regret began to creep over him. Why had he left the dear old place? Again and again he found himself looking back over his shoulder to the points of advantage he had given up. Those regretful glances divided his energy and disrupted his peace of mind. In his stronger, saner moments he felt ashamed of this weakness; but there it was!

And there it is with many of us—that tendency to look back to yesterday's decision with the futile wish that we could undo it; that wish to retrace the paths by which we worked out yesterday's problem and to wonder whether we could have done it otherwise; that inclination to spoil today's happiness by letting in the yelping pack of yesterday's hounding worries and regrets. Such are the very common versions of this tendency to look back when we should be looking ahead.

The control of the backward look is one of the chief secrets of personal power and happiness.

The man of action weighs the evidence, balances the issues, reaches a decision—then dismisses it. The situation is declined, or the step is taken, or the contract is signed —then the gate is firmly and finally closed. The successful man looks forward to opportunities, not back to settled questions.

Life, of course, is not a succession of time-tight compartments. The past does flow into the present, bearing with it the wealth of memory. By capitalizing on the experiences of our yesterdays we enlarge the enjoyment of our todays. But in so doing we must learn how to be selective —taking over the assets of the past while leaving out its liabilities.

I have been talking as if this control of the backward look were purely a matter of man's own will power. But it is not. God helps to blot out the bedeviling past. How? For one thing, God helps us to advance from remorse to repentance. It does not do any good just to remember sins which we cannot undo. To sit and brood over them tortures the mind without cleansing the conscience.

But when we bring God into our situation, he lifts us out of our self-centered remorse. He breaks the closed circle in which we sit alone with our errors and sins, thinking how they have hurt us. He turns us from worldly grief to spiritual grief.

We should remember the distinction which Paul drew when he said: "Godly grief produces a repentance that leads to salvation and brings no regret, but worldly grief produces death."

Some years ago a young man committed a very serious wrong. He was filled with remorse. His future seemed ruined. His father was a highly respected leading man of the community. The father learned of his son's misdeed on a Sunday morning. At luncheon he asked the young fellow to meet him in the study after the meal. There the father said something like this: "My son, I cannot condone your sin. It would be wrong for me to do so. You have done a thing which cannot be fully repaired. But I am in this with you. I can and I will bear for you the ill desert which judgment demands."

Like that father, our heavenly Father identifies himself with his erring children. The scars of the sin may remain, but the loving relationship also remains. Forgiveness is the experience of having one's sins swallowed up in a great engulfing love. And that is what God does with the past we cannot undo.

❖❖❖❖❖❖❖❖❖❖

THAT'S HUMAN NATURE

Consider how much cold water has been poured on the world's ideals through the spouting of these words: "You can't change human nature."

For instance, a civic reform begins to stir a city. Earnest citizens arouse themselves to cleanse the community of vice and corruption. Then the cynics come forth with their sneering comment, "You can't change human nature"; and the reform movement is left limping halfheartedly toward an ignoble end.

Again, millions of youth are enlisted in a war with the promise of insuring a peaceful world. They struggle, they die, many come back crippled, and the rest return to meet the pessimistic prattle: "But after all you can't change human nature; man is a fighting animal, always has been, always will be; therefore wars are inevitable." And succumbing to such skepticism, the survivors of one war begin to prepare for another, and international peace machinery like the United Nations is weakened.

The late Benito Mussolini, whose so-called dynamic realism for a time impressed his own people and many of ours, declared, "There is no revolution which can change human nature." Holding this belief, he banked on humanity's worst elements, capitalized its greeds, developed its deceitfulness, until at last he became the victim of its brutality and was left hanging by the heels, reviled by his own revolutionists, whose nature certainly he had not changed.

But this pessimism about the possible improvement of human nature runs counter to the convictions of our leading psychologists, philosophers, and religions.

Professor Hocking, formerly of Harvard, asserts that human nature is the most plastic part of the living world. Of all animals, it is man in whom heredity counts for least and conscious building forces for most. Consider that man's infancy is longest, his instincts least fixed, his brain most unfinished at birth. Man differs from other living beings in the vim and deliberate intention of his self-shaping. Hocking sums up by saying: "To anyone who asserts as a dogma, 'Human nature never changes,' it is fair to reply, 'It is human nature to change itself.'"

And when we turn to the sphere of religion, we find the great ethnic faiths have spoken ill of original human nature, but they never despair of its possibilities. Our own Hebrew-Christian faith holds ever before men the promise of improvement up toward the image of God. The prevailing attitude of the Old Testament prophets is in line with Isaiah's passage:

Come now, let us reason together,
  says the Lord:
though your sins are like scarlet,
  they shall be as white as snow.

Hugh Price Hughes, a long-time missionary in London's slums, was once challenged by an atheist to a public debate on religious faith. Hughes said he would accept, provided each debater could bring some products of his work. He was ready to exhibit any number of ex-drunkards, purified prostitutes, reformed thieves. The atheist had no such results to show, so the debate never came off. Religion does change lives.

Among all these assertions about men made over, consider this one by Paul: "Seeing that ye have put off the old man with his deeds; and have put on the new man, which is renewed in knowledge after the image of him that created him" (K.J.V.).

Paul is reminding us that remaking ourselves is a continuing process. In my boyhood community revival services were held each winter and usually a number would be converted. Then during the summer some would "backslide." (I haven't used that word much lately because in New York my people don't get far enough ahead to slide back.) Their wills had been converted but their tastes had not. And they slipped back to what they liked to do.

Sometimes we are converted in our passions but not in our pocketbooks. We are decent but we are stingy. Sometimes we are converted in our religious sentiments but not in our politics. We are pious in our prayers but vote our prejudices.

The Lenten season is the traditional time for spiritual overhauling and renewal. But why wait for Lent?

BETTER WITH AGE

In the book of Ecclesiastes we find this statement: "Better is the end of a thing than the beginning thereof" (K.J.V.) .

If the writer means that the end of a thing is more important than its beginning, then I for one would readily admit that he is right. Certainly it is better to have a thing turn out well than to have it start well.

But as a matter of fact, the end of a thing is not always better than its beginning. A career may start well and end miserably. Japan's war with America began with a victory for her at Pearl Harbor and ended with utter failure. Therefore, when we read the statement, "Better is the end of a thing than the beginning thereof," we say, "That depends."

First of all, if a thing is to end better than it began, it must be based on values that last. Keats said, "A thing of beauty is a joy forever." Understanding persons recognize this truth in the realm of art. The frescoes of Michelangelo and the "Sistine Madonna" of Raphael are prized even more today than when they were first produced. Yes, we admit that time adds to the beauty and value of some things.

But when we turn to the realm of our own lives, we do not seem to feel that they grow better with age. We picture Father Time as a grim reaper who cuts down the grass of the field.

Time withers the fresh vigor of youth, it saps our strength, it dims our eye. It lures us with hopes and then dissolves our dreams like the mirage of the desert. Time may enhance a work of art, but it seems to spoil the art of work.

Is it possible to make our own living such a work of art that it grows better with age? Well, that depends on

21

whether we learn to live with and for the values that last. We start to school at about the age of six, and during the next twelve to sixteen years we have spread before us in condensed survey the findings of the ages in the various fields of human endeavor. We learn, or should learn, what has been tried and tested. Thus we profit by the experience of the past.

Thus man differs from a dog. The dog of today goes through the same tricks as the dog of two thousand years ago. Dogs cannot avail themselves of the wisdom of their ancestors, but man can. That is why we go to school.

But study in school is only the beginning. We must go on learning lasting values by living. The late Karl Stolz of Hartford Seminary divided adult life into four periods. The period from twenty-three to thirty-five he called the period of adjustment. From thirty-five to fifty-five, the period of achievement. From fifty-five to sixty-five, the period of conservation. And from sixty-five on, the period of retirement.

But retirement does not necessarily mean retreat. Like a good general, a person may retire his forces on some fronts in order to advance on others. Some of the world's best work has been done by those who were too old to get a job in the business field. Immanuel Kant was seventy-four when he wrote his monumental *Metaphysics of Ethics*. Goethe was past eighty when he finished *Faust*.

Once after a crushing political defeat William Gladstone rose to speak in the House of Commons with a buoyant smile, saying, "Time is on our side." So it is with all of us who live for lasting values.

GIVING GOD A CHANCE

Suppose, as you are reading this, we should learn that our nation had been attacked by a hostile government. It would be tragic, just as it was some fifteen years ago when we were dumbfounded by the news of Pearl Harbor. Yet, though horror-stricken, we would be jerked out of the petty anxieties which now bedevil us. Awful as were the last war and the losses we sustained in the Korean conflict, we were not looking for books on peace of mind during those days.

It was after the guns were silenced, when we leaped back into our self-centeredness, that we feverishly sought for books on how to be happy and peaceful and unafraid. It is after a war is over, that we look back to the time when we were caught up in a patriot's zeal and picture it on the screen under the title: "The Best Years of Our Lives." Must we wait for another war to lift us out of our pettiness and worries?

Or suppose we should fall head over heels in love. We have a saying: "All the world loves a lover." Why? Because when a person is deeply in love, he becomes more lovable. He may do silly things. He may make a fool of himself in many little ways. But, nevertheless, he is lovable because he forgets himself and ceases to be always calculating, always looking out for "Me first." Must we wait for romantic love to give us the peace and joy which come from surrendering our hearts?

Why can we not this day surrender our wills to God, as we yield our hearts to our country in time of war or to a loved one in time of love? God gave us this country that we love. God's love made possible these personal loves which are so dear to us.

Why not, then, respond to God's goodness and love by opening our hearts to him and giving him the chance as sovereign Lord to take over these lives of ours? Then we would know what Paul meant by "the peace of God, which passeth all understanding" (K.J.V.).

And after we have opened the door, why not give God a chance to stay with us by reading his Word more regularly? It has been said that if we are to endure dark days, we must do one of two things: either stop thinking or stop and think.

And I might add that it makes a great difference *where* we stop and think. If the only times during which we stop and think are after we have read the reports of corruption and crime, we are bound to be depressed. If we are to keep up our morale, we must balance the bad news of men with the good news of God. Instead of trembling with fear by thinking so much about what the Communists and other enemies may do *to* us, let us turn to the Bible and think what God has done *for* us.

Now look around you. Why not give God a chance in your family? That is where you really bring your religion home to yourself. We know what we mean when we say that a thing has "come home to us." We mean that it has really come to count with us, that it has "gotten under the skin."

In my grandfather's home was hung a framed motto, "Christ Is the Head of This House." Perhaps that was old fashioned, but it stood for something that should never go out of fashion.

John Ruskin was right when he said that the history of a nation is not to be read in its battlefields but in its homes. A good home is one that is good to come back to, one in which love helps us to pull ourselves together after the distracting and competing experiences of the day, one where a listening and sympathetic circle invites us to unpack our hearts with words.

Where is there a lovelier sight than a house lighted up at the Christmas season—red wreaths in the windows, a decorated tree in the corner, a family gathered before a glowing fire. God gave us these homes. Let's give God a chance with them.

II

When Fears Invade

❖❖❖❖❖❖❖❖❖❖❖❖

EASTER

From coast to coast multitudes gather in Easter dawn services. It is right that Easter should be welcomed at sunrise. The earliest gospel record of the Resurrection, that given by Mark, has this statement, "They came unto the sepulchre at the rising of the sun" (K.J.V.). Easter is a festival of dawn.

Jesus Christ did not originate the belief that life is too great for the grave. That conviction is found among the most primitive people and persists among the most cultured. But what Christ by his career and resurrection did do was, as Paul said, to bring "life and immortality to light through the gospel" (K.J.V.). Christ transformed death from a sunset to a sunrise.

I should believe in immortality even if I had never read the stories of Easter morning. When I look at the physical world, my reason leads me to believe that life goes beyond the body.

There is something that makes this universe go. It is not dead. It is throbbing with life. The mysterious force called life is touching the roots of the trees outside my door. The promise of spring's resurging life is in the air.

The flowers feel it. The birds feel it. We feel it, for the

26

life in us is a part of that central force which surges through all creation, covering the ground with green, clothing the trees with foliage, pecking its way through the shell of the egg, swinging the stars through space.

Like Don Marquis, beloved author and playwright of a few years ago, I believe that this life force is imperishable, for the simple reason that if it stopped, the result would be nothingness, and a complete state of nothingness cannot be imagined.

And I feel that some of this universal, imperishable, ongoing life is in me. How it came to me I do not know. To be sure, that spark of life was passed on to me by my parents at birth, but that power of generation is a mystery.

It is a mystery, too, where the seat of life is. It might seem to be in the brain, for a blow on the head or a clot in the brain can cause paralysis and death. But even if the brain be the seat of life, it is not the source of it. The brain does not secrete thought as the liver produces bile. It only transmits a force which appears to flow through it.

And this life process, which flows through our bodies, preserves our personal identity through all our bodily changes. Does it not, therefore, seem possible that personality can survive the extreme bodily changes of the grave?

Yes, life is more than brain. These lives of ours presuppose a vaster whole of which we are a part. And when I consider human personality, possessed of a spirit which is so much more than the body, my reason tells me that life is too great for the grave and death cannot hold the soul.

But mere logic is cold comfort when loved ones are taken. Moreover, when death strikes close to home, it stuns the mind so that we do not think clearly. And then comes Christ to bring our minds out of the dusk into the dawn.

And when we live close enough to Christ to catch his spirit, our belief in immortality is illumined with radiant hope. Jesus did not prepare for death as a man getting ready for retirement, but as one preparing for a larger work.

Jesus showed his mastery of death both by the way he faced it and by the way he emerged from it. And the Easter events convince me that Christ did emerge from the grave. I cannot account for the church without the Resurrection.

When I was thirteen, I was riding home from school one night and had to cross a stream which the rain had raised. Darkness had fallen, and my horse refused to enter the rushing water. Suddenly a farmer opened the door of a farmhouse on the other side of the stream. From the open door came a path of lamplight. In that path of light my horse and I took courage and crossed the flooded creek.

So Christ opened the door on the other side of death's stream and "brought life and immortality to light."

GOD'S SECRET SERVICE

It is usually not a pleasant feeling to know we are being watched by persons we cannot see. During past years I have been in a number of countries ruled by dictators. In those lands we were pretty sure our movements were observed by secret police, and we did not like it.

In fact, most of us do not like to be exposed too much

even to the eyes of the curious, though they be not hostile. Personally I should not care to be hypnotized and used as an exhibit in a demonstration before a crowd. It is a mark of refinement to wish one's privacy respected.

But while we dislike to be watched by the hostile and the curious, there are times when we crave to have friendly eyes upon us. The little boy, when he is learning to turn somersaults, cries, "Look, daddy," and he does it better when his father's encouraging gaze is on him. The little girl, tossing feverishly on her bed, can go to sleep better when she knows that mother is sitting near enough to watch over her. Recent experiences have convinced me that there are more American children left hungry for love than for food.

And how about adults? I think of a schoolteacher whose father died when she was three. Growing up in a family circle dominated by older stepsisters, she was deprived of normal parental love. Somewhat starved for affection, she married a man who turned out to be no good and, after being supported by her for some years, ran away with another woman.

And now this teacher tries bravely to keep up her spirits during the day for the sake of her pupils, but after hours she finds the loneliness of her four walls almost unbearable. Yes, although we like the privacy which shelters us from prying and hostile eyes, we also long for kindly and sympathetic eyes to save us from our loneliness.

Oscar Wilde told in his book *De Profundis* that when he was being led handcuffed between two policemen from prison to the Court of Bankruptcy, a friend of his waited for him in the dreary corridor. As the prisoner passed, this friend gravely raised his hat. Wilde wrote later that this gesture comforted and moved him more than all his philosophizing. He said: "The memory of this little, lovely, silent act of love has unsealed for me all the wells of pity."

Even our Lord himself craved the fellowship of an understanding group. In my opinion, Jesus did not choose his disciples merely that he might train them as teachers to carry forth his message and work. I think he also desired them for their comradeship. From the curious and hostile crowds Jesus repeatedly withdrew to the company of the little group which understood him.

During that last trying week in Jerusalem, Jesus is supposed to have spent his evenings in the fellowship of his closest friends at Bethany. And on the fateful night of the Last Supper, he said to his disciples: "With desire I have desired to eat this passover with you before I suffer" (K.J.V.) . And he showed his gratitude for their comradeship when he added a moment later: "Ye are they which have continued with me in my temptations." The Son of Man, like the sons of men, needed fellowship both human and divine.

After World War II a refugee from Nazi Germany said the difference between the land he left and our America to which he had come could be symbolized by one word— "doorbells." Over there at the sound of the doorbell, inmates of a house would hide, suspecting the police. Here the ring of the doorbell signals the coming of the friendly delivery boy or the cheery neighbor. We are surrounded by allies—families, friends, neighbors.

And think a little further. I am not endowed with any special mystical perception, and I hope I am not sentimental, but I feel the mother who watched over me in my infancy, who went with me in spirit when I left home for school, is still with me at certain moments when my mind is properly attuned.

Well, whether we believe it or not, the Scripture asserts that "we are compassed about with so great a cloud of witnesses" (K.J.V.) —those persons of faith whose bodies have left the earth but whose spirits still form an invisible fellowship.

We know that governments have their secret police. But God also has a Secret Service—and its members are allies, not spies.

❖❖❖❖❖❖❖❖❖❖❖❖

FINGERPRINTS OR FOOTPRINTS

Fingerprints are a means by which we track our criminals. Footprints are marks by which we follow our heroes. It is thought sentimental by many to quote the old-fashioned lines of Longfellow:

> Lives of great men all remind us
> We can make our lives sublime,
> And, departing, leave behind us
> Footprints on the sands of time.

On the other hand it is considered clever to detect the fingerprints of evil around us. We have talked so much about the badness of men, that we expect to find the sordid rather than the noble. And it is the law of life that we see the traits for which we look.

It was against this natural tendency that Paul warned: "Be not overcome of evil, but overcome evil with good" (K.J.V.). At that dark time the lives of many were de-

31

pressed to the point of making things worse than they were or needed to be. They, like ourselves, needed to look from the fingerprints of evil to the footprints of good.

For one thing, we should look from the fingerprints to the footprints in order to keep from getting a falsely exaggerated idea of the forces of evil. In a struggle, if one opponent can get the other downright afraid of him, he has begun the process of overcoming. And one of the best ways of creating this fear is by repeated suggestions of his own strength.

This was the principle on which Hitler worked to intimidate and soften the Nazis' neighbors. This same method of propaganda has been used by the Soviet Union to impress its satellites and others with Russia's resources.

And today we in America are prone to see some of our domestic dangers too darkly. We talk so much about juvenile delinquency that we may come to think all boys and girls are bad. The cleverness of criminals is so played up that organized crime seems to be more powerful than the law.

While there is much to make us think that evil wins over good, a wider reading of history reveals that the footprints of goodness give evidence of progress and purpose.

My old teacher Charles A. Beard, a great historian of Columbia University, when asked what lessons he had learned from history, said that he had learned four: First, although the mills of the gods grind slowly, yet they grind exceeding small. Second, those whom the gods are about to destroy they first make mad. Third, when it gets dark enough you can see stars. Fourth, the bee fertilizes the flower that it robs.

Ponder these four conclusions of the renowned historian: the slow but inevitable working of divine justice, the suicidal futility of anger, the emergence of stars in the night, and the fertilization of life through the stings of sacrifice. Do these not point to footprints which lead from pessimism to hope?

Let's be realistic in our view of good and evil. There is a popular Pollyanna preaching today which asserts that if we just think things are all right, so they will be. This makes religion too easy.

On the other hand, we can also fool ourselves by seeing things too darkly. Let's face the facts, but try to see all the facts. And when we do, we discover what Paul learned, "Where sin increased, grace abounded all the more."

One of the most fascinating departments of the Federal Bureau of Investigation is the one which contains the fingerprints of criminals. It was organized primarily for the purpose of identifying men and women whose contempt for our laws resulted in their arrest. Fingerprints were regarded as a stigma. Now there is another department of fingerprints in the offices of the F.B.I. These fingerprints represent thousands of honest citizens who voluntarily submitted themselves to the process. In the event of death or accident, they may be readily identified by their families or friends. What began as a system for trailing evildoers led to protective measures for law-abiding people.

So often evil has inspired the good to overcome it. Without ravishing fires we might never have improved the old hand pump of our forefathers.

The best way to overcome evil is to make goodness more attractive. Evil is driven out as darkness is driven out, for evil is the absence of goodness as darkness is the absence of light. We cannot dispel darkness with a fan or a sword. We turn on the light and the shadows flee. Likewise we turn on our goodness and evil disappears. We can reach for that switch right now, wherever we are.

SAFETY FIRST---WHERE?

Many of us want to play everything safe. And yet we would not be here in peace and plenty if the Pilgrim Fathers and George Washington had "played safe."

The late historian James Truslow Adams complained that in one hundred and fifty years we have changed from a land of opportunity to a land of safety first. And a writer recently observed that "when a young fellow comes looking for a job, his first interest is likely not to be what the chances of promotion are, but what kind of pension he will get forty years hence."

My contacts on many college campuses each year convince me that such comments are a bit overcolored. I do not believe American youth have lost the spirit of adventure. But the trouble is that we are becoming security-conscious in the wrong places.

The irony of our search for security is that when we arrange our work and livelihood so that we no longer venture for great things, we gamble on small things. That is one reason why gambling on horse races and dog races, on numbers and sports, has so greatly increased in our time.

Also, while we are trying to play safe in our careers, we increase our risks by recklessness in motor cars and seek thrills in false excitement. You see, our natures crave some elements of chance. If every outcome were sure, life would be deadly. There would be no place for faith and hope and love. But let's take our chances in the right places.

Surely we need safety campaigns to prevent accidents in our homes, our factories, and on our roads. "Safety First" is a good slogan in handling tools and cars, but not in handling talents and lives.

While brave men lose their lives in pioneering new paths, others let their spirits die inch by inch in play at little games. Our generation is in the grip of the gambling mania, but all too much it is a taking of chances on small things rather than big issues. Thus we lose our real lives.

Some who would save their lives lose them by trying too hard to conserve their energy. We cannot hoard life as we can money. When a person tries to be a miser of his health, he usually makes himself miserable. People who are constantly watching for symptoms and coddling their complaints become slaves to the thermometer and fugitives from germs, living below par and often dying before their time.

In the mental realm this principle of losing by trying to save is even more apparent. The intelligent student does not say to himself, "Since I shall need all my mental strength in my career after college I shall conserve it during these four years." Some students, it must be admitted, do seem to act on this principle, but it does not work! Mental talents, if buried and not used, tend to deteriorate. Whoever would save his memory by not using it, will lose it.

Our emotional nature reveals still more clearly the fallacy of trying to save by conservation. In a recent book of fiction, one of the characters, a sheltered woman, asks that she not be made to see other people's hardships any more often than necessary because sympathy puts such a strain on her emotions.

Some people avoid funerals for the reason that they do not want their feelings harassed. Many do not want the pulpit to deal with unpleasant things like war and poverty. They prefer to hear only of pleasant things which will not trouble them. But remember, the field that is never plowed by any furrows or harrowed by any discs becomes hard and unproductive. So it is with life.

When we keep ourselves shut off from things which would stir our sympathies, when we hold ourselves back

35

from others lest we be taken in by them, we find the soil of our minds becoming harder and the boundaries of our affection becoming narrower. Love and sympathy are dissipated not by use but by disuse. Thus, in trying to save ourselves from being spent, we lose ourselves.

One whom millions call the Master of life laid down a principle that is worth pondering. Here it is: "Whoever would save his life will lose it." Life has to be spent. The question is, what will a man give in exchange for his soul?

❧✥✥✥✥✥✥✥✥✥✥✥✥❧

SECURITY IN HEIGHT

For many years I have been haunted by the prayer of the Psalmist: "Lead me to the rock that is higher than I" (K.J.V.). This prayer of the Hebrew singer was born out of experiences which most of us sooner or later share. The Psalmist felt himself in a danger zone and was looking for security.

And who does not feel himself in some danger zone? Some may be in fear of physical danger. Others may feel a sense of economic insecurity, the fear of what may happen when they pass the deadline of employability. And all thoughtful people are troubled about the perils which threaten the world's peace.

We, like the Psalmist, desire to escape the danger zones of life. In his day there was security in height. In those early days of Palestinian fighting, the high mountain strongholds were the easiest to defend. Modern warfare has seemed to accentuate the advantage of altitude.

Aviators know the tactical value of getting above the op-
posing plane.

In living as in fighting, one advantage of altitude is
security. If we are to keep our heads clear, our hearts
clean, and our bodies secure, we must live above certain
danger zones.

Consider the security given by high thoughts. High
thinking lifts us above the attacks of petty insults and irritating slights which bedevil our lower moods. High
thoughts give us security from the ravages of little worries
which sap our energies. They deliver us from the in-
vasions of envy which so frequently destroy our peace
of mind.

In the early days of the Southern Confederacy, General
Robert E. Lee was severely criticized by General Whiting.
It might have been expected that Lee would wait for a
time when he could get even. A day came when President
Jefferson Davis asked General Lee to come for consultation.

Davis wanted to know what Lee thought of General
Whiting. Without hesitation, Lee commended Whiting in
high terms. An officer present drew Lee aside to suggest
that he must not know what unkind things Whiting had
been saying about him. Lee answered: "I understood that
the President desired to know my opinion of Whiting, not
Whiting's opinion of me."

Think, too, of the security given by high tastes as well
as by high thoughts. High tastes preserve us from the
lure of the vulgar, the clamor of the cheap, the baubles of
Vanity Fair.

Remember also that high standards, like high thoughts
and tastes, lift us out of certain danger zones. Some persons
live on a plane of conduct so lofty that the compromises
and expediencies of others do not affect them. I can well
imagine what the businessman is up against when he tries

to maintain high ethical standards in competition with those who will stoop to any trick to turn a deal. And yet I know of men who have established noble reputations and large enterprises in various professions and businesses primarily because of their high standards.

They have avoided the danger zones of low competition, somewhat as we have helped to lessen traffic accidents by eliminating grade crossings on our highways. They travel at a different level from those who are moving at cross purposes.

While the Psalmist's petition may have arisen out of the desire for security, it does not end on that note. It is the prayer of a climber. Every attainment becomes a vantage point from which the climber glimpses a higher range of desired achievement, and he is restless to keep climbing.

But this aspiration toward the higher rock does more than increase security and enlarge the vision of life's possibilities. It begins to appear after a time that the elusive ideal helps in the doing of the practical real.

Consider the case of King David, with whom this psalm is linked. David had four great aims in his royal career. He desired to win his nation's wars, to secure his nation's independence, to build his nation's capital at Jerusalem, and then to crown that capital with a great temple of God.

He did the first three, but not the fourth. Yet may it not be that he did better the three things he could do because he wanted to do a fourth thing which was beyond his reach? It is a law of life that our best work is done when we are haunted by the desire for something beyond our grasp.

III

When the World Is Too Much with Us

❖❖❖❖❖❖❖❖❖❖❖❖

OUR UNWRITTEN LAWS

In some railroad cars there are signs prohibiting smoking. But in the churches where we worship no such signs are needed. Why? It is an unwritten law that worshipers do not smoke in the house of God. Something in the nature of the building, something in the character of the worshipers, makes it unnecessary to post such regulations in a sanctuary.

Sermons, however eloquent, do not receive open applause. It is an unwritten law that we do not clap our hands in our more dignified places of worship.

Or consider the home. Out in the business world hours and wages are strictly regulated by law. But there is no wage-and-hour schedule in the labors of family devotion. There is no ceiling to the cost of service a mother will pay for a sick child. If death breaks up a home and the property adjustments are thrown into court, then there are laws which apportion the share of a widow or a child. But as long as a home is a going institution, it is run by unwritten laws.

When children are little, they pull no oar in the boat.

They are only passengers, a precious cargo, to be sure, but very exacting. And when parents become aged and infirm, they often become passengers to be carried. Yet dutiful sons and daughters do not desert helpless fathers and mothers. Homes are held together by unwritten laws.

Let us look at society at large. Some of our actions can be regulated by statutes, such as the terms of our employment in factories, the speed of driving on public highways, and so on. On the other hand, some of the things we do should be outside the reach of law. Such is the right to worship God or the right to think for ourselves. But in between the actions controlled by statute and the rights to be kept absolutely free is a third region of conduct, once discussed by Lord Moulton, the English jurist. This third realm of action Lord Moulton called the domain of "obedience to the unenforceable." It covers all those acts we do when there is no one but ourselves to make us do them, all those restraints which we observe when there is no statute law to hold us back.

Let us pause a moment to ponder this obedience to the unenforceable. This is a land of free speech, but does that fact warrant any of us saying publicly everything that comes into his head? No, for a wise person keeps some thoughts to himself.

Suppose he is a teacher. He has to consider the capacities and sensibilities of the pupils under his care. Or suppose he is a preacher. The freedom of the pulpit exempts him from legal restrictions, but not from the restraints of gentlemanly courtesy or Christian charity. As a minister I feel that it would be a sin against fair play to say certain things from my pulpit (where men cannot talk back to me) which I should feel free to say in private conversation.

Forty-three years ago, when the ship "Titanic" struck an iceberg and went to a watery grave, the passengers observed the rule "women and children first." No written law required the men to stand back while the women and children went to the lifeboats. No force compelled such conduct. But by the unwritten law of chivalry those gentlemen remained gentlemen, even to the edge of death. This was a classic example of obedience to the unenforceable.

And why is this obedience to the unenforceable so socially important? Because our freedom, our virtue, and our sacred honor depend on it. Unless we the people obey the unwritten laws of right conduct, when there is no one but ourselves to enforce them, then the lust for lawmaking will spread until all conduct is more or less regulated by laws, and the totalitarianism of the dictators will have replaced the democracy of free peoples. Do we want all our daily doings dictated by governmental overlords? Then we must hold the lordship of our lives as a sacred trust to be exercised under the Lord of all life.

Furthermore, men are made good by spirit and not by law. There is no goose-stepping goodness. Unless we live up to the spirit of the good life, we shall live down to the level of mental slavery and moral mediocrity.

◆◇◆◇◆◇◆◇◆◇◆

BEING GOOD IN BAD PLACES

So often it is said, "When a place is bad, get out of it." Sometimes the best thing to do in a bad situation is to pick up and leave.

But as a rule righteous people do not save a situation by withdrawing from it. I may pull out of a firm whose aims and methods run counter to my conscience, but if I am to make a living I cannot easily withdraw from the whole business system. I may feel impelled to leave a political party, but if I am to have any influence in civic life, I must vote in some party. And unless good men go into politics, what hope is there for better government?

We are human beings living in social systems, and we cannot cut ourselves off from all groups which do things contrary to our consciences. Being good in the kind of world we inhabit is a tough assignment. Some say it is impossible.

Edna Ferber in her book *So Big* tells of a young woman teacher who was so baffled by the difficulties of her situation that she wanted to run away. An old Dutch housewife said to her: "You can't run away from life, missy; you can't run far enough."

The temptations which threaten a person's ideals begin even before he gets out into the world on his own. Many a student faces in school some of the fiercest moral struggles of his life. The change from the parental rooftree to the freedom of the campus is one of the most severe tests of character. It comes at a time when the animal spirits of youth are at the full. To keep one's purity and temperance and integrity on a modern campus is not easy.

And the test of being good in bad places may come even before college age is reached. Not all our homes are good places for growing children. When a home is poisoned by the presence of a bad parent, or is pervaded by a materialistic atmosphere, or is weakened by deceit and distrust— then the home itself is a hard place in which to be good.

The first thing it takes to be good in a bad place is conviction. During the Senate Crime Commission's investigation a few years ago, a U.S. senator said that one trouble of our time is that so many people have no strong convictions about right and wrong. They never take a firm stand. We never know where and when we can count them.

But a good person's convictions must be clear as well as strong. Here is the difference, as I see it, between stubbornness and steadfastness. A stubborn person has strong convictions, as a mule may take a stand and hold it. But in the eyes of a balky mule I have never seen much light of intelligence. Of course, I never have had much personal association with mules, but I have known many of their relatives.

A steadfast person has a reason for his convictions. His mind is not closed by prejudice or bigotry. It is open to reason, yet firm in purpose.

The soldiers of King Charles I said of George Fox, the founder of the Quakers, that he was "stiff as a tree and pure as a bell." What a tribute from a man's enemies! Fox could not be bent. In prison after prison he was beaten and bruised, but he held to his convictions, illumined by an inner light which so shone before men that many came "to see his good works."

Ah, that's the point. The person who can keep his virtues under temptation, who can keep sweet when things go sour, who can keep his courage when others are giving up—that person shows that he "has something." Others see it and want it.

Remember, goodness can be as contagious as badness. Yes, even more so.

BIGNESS OR GREATNESS

To add size without strength is not real growth. A boy may grow up so fast that he is not as strong as his tall body might lead us to expect. He has to wait until his strength catches up with his size.

Further, bodies may add weight after they have stopped growing. That is a subject we think about at the table three times a day, so why discuss it here? Suffice it to remind ourselves that growing up is more than merely getting bigger.

Henry Hough, editor of the *Vineyard Gazette* of Edgartown, Mass., once pointed out that too many modern people think of things that are small as merely the early and imperfect stage of things that should be bigger and better. They seem to think that being concerned with small things is a failure of ambition. He said: "I believe that a big world is not necessarily a grown-up world and that the values of life are not measured by any standard of size. . . . I know of no vastness of enterprise that can outweigh a single human heart."

In the jazz era of the 1920's someone remarked about the current American mood: "Whatever is small wants to be big, whatever is poor wants to be rich, whatever is slow wants to be fast, whatever is wants to be more so!" Yes, we did have a sort of addition complex, a cult of size and speed.

We must still beware lest we mistake bigness for greatness. The Soviet Union has more people and also more land than the United States; but after seeing Russia I am convinced that ours is the far stronger and greater nation.

We Americans pride ourselves in doing things in a big way. When we visit little countries like Holland or Denmark, we tend to look a bit condescendingly on their plots of ground and their methods of organization. But when we note what some of those European farmers produce on their small acreage, we wake up to the unrealized possibilities resident in our soil and to some aspects of our wastefulness in its use. As the earth becomes more crowded and the demands rise for higher standards of living, we must learn to cultivate small areas more intensively.

If we are to grow up into real strength, we must regain our respect for the importance of little things and the cultivation of the local and the personal. A good mother intensively cultivates her domestic domain. Whether she has one child or eight, each one is uniquely personal and infinitely precious.

A mother makes allowance for the peculiar temperament of Tom and studies how to strengthen the weak will of Jim. She gives herself to that little circle even though she may see other women of no more talent spreading their influence across the pages of the press.

With our improved methods of work, mothers no longer need to consume their whole energy in household drudgery. And many a mother now is able to exert wide influence in public life. But no substitute has yet been devised for personal mothering care. And if our youth are to grow up and become strong in spirit, we must combine this principle of local cultivation with our large world outlooks.

It was said of Robert Browning that one of his eyes was nearsighted and the other was farsighted. When he wanted to see a distant object, he opened one eye and closed the other. When he desired to see things near at hand, he reversed the eye movement. Thus, as someone said, the great poet "saw the long and the short of it."

We need Browning's bifocal vision today. We must see the large outlooks, for we have to live as world citizens. But we must also cultivate local loyalties.

We must develop personal godly attitudes. In our changing world, attitudes are more important than skills. The skills we learn today may be of little use ten years hence. The weapons we are now producing in such vast volume may be lying in rubbish heaps after this spurt is over.

But attitudes are permanently effective. Training in character fits individuals and nations to handle any kind of power from the human hand to atomic fission.

❖❖❖❖❖❖❖❖❖❖❖

OUR RIGHTS

We all want our rights. And America's Declaration of Independence asserts that we have certain inalienable rights, such as life, liberty, and the pursuit of happiness.

Consider the right to life itself. I have a right to life, and yet there are certain conditions under which I cannot exercise it. Suppose that I am on a raft adrift in the ocean with a dozen comrades and a supply of food so meager that it must be strictly rationed. In the night I awake while the others are asleep, and in the agony of my gnawing hunger I say to myself, "I have a right to live," and thereupon proceed to take more than my share of the food supply. Such conduct would ostracize me from the society of decent men.

Or suppose I am a soldier on picket duty. Danger approaches. I say, "I have a right to life," and desert my post to seek safety in flight. Such behavior would receive quick action through court martial.

Yes, I have a right to life, but even this most basic of all rights must be exercised with fairness to others, or I am in danger of forfeiting their lives and my own.

Or consider the inalienable right of liberty. This is a land of free speech. Am I therefore free to say anything which comes to my mind? Well, I happen to be a minister, and I pride myself that my pulpit is about as free as any. And yet there are some things which common sense tells me I am not free to say in my pulpit.

Likewise, the teacher in our free schools is not at liberty to say anything which comes into her head. She must consider what is due the children in her charge. Yes, whoever we are and wherever we are, we must exercise our freedom with fairness to others. Such is their due.

Another freedom which we stress is the right of free enterprise. A person should very properly be free to advance according to his own ability. We are not all equal in ability. Some are five-talent men and some are one-talent men. It is unfair to the five-talent man to hold him back to the pace of his one-talent brother.

Jesus did not advocate such a procedure in his parable of the talents. Such a restriction would kill initiative and reduce life to dull regimentation. But on the other hand, the man of superior talents, who should be free to get ahead, should also take care not to block the road of his weaker brother.

In a horse race, the horse which gets ahead takes the inside track and thereby gains the advantage of crowding his competitors from the rail. In the race of life the talented man does things more easily and quickly than his less able fellows. But his superior ability should make him more sensitive to the rights of others and more careful not to block their way. For, remember, the race of life is not a horse race.

The Epistle to the Hebrews describes the race of life thus: "Seeing we also are compassed about with so great a cloud of witnesses, . . . let us run with patience the race that is set before us, looking unto Jesus the author and finisher of our faith." (K.J.V.)

This is very different from the horse-race concept of our competitive living, which could be characterized thus: "Seeing that we are compassed about with a great company of competitors, let us run with feverish haste the race that is set before us, looking unto our rivals that we may crowd them from the rail and beat them to the post."

And what about our inalienable right to the pursuit of happiness? No one can long be happy all by himself. Life is a game and the zest comes in playing fair. The fellow who cheats spoils the fun for others and eventually for himself. The most joyous tennis player I ever encountered had only one leg. He played a good game and most of all he played the man. He did not ask the other players to pay for his handicap.

I have a right to pursue happiness provided I do not ask my wife or my child or my friends or the state to pay for it. In short, our rights must be earned by our responsibilities.

HAVING A SENSE OF HONOR

A sense of honor is not one of our physical instincts. Yet it is often stronger than these.

Hunger, for instance, is a primary instinctive drive. A man will do almost anything to satisfy his bodily hunger. Almost, but not quite. The histories of battlefields and besieged garrisons and exploring parties repeat the record of men who suffer the agony of gnawing hunger rather than break over the allotted rations and poach from the common store. What keeps a person from stealing out of the common store of his companions? Fear? Not always. It is something more—a sense of honor.

Sex is another instinctive desire, so strong that some psychologists interpret it as conditioning almost all conduct. And to be sure, it has turned Caesars into silly slaves, duped Napoleons, and torn countless homes up by the roots. But men have found a self-mastery able to subdue this tumultuous passion and to preserve the purity of the home. What is it that restrains the sex urge? Fear? Not always. There is also this sense of honor.

Love of money is another impulse so powerful that it has been called the root of all evil. Many would have us believe that the economic motive overshadows all others. Yet we think of Spinoza, the philosopher, living in Holland, grinding lenses for a living while he pondered his great thoughts of God. Louis XIV of France offered him a pension and patronage if he would dedicate even one book to his majesty, but Spinoza did not approve of Louis XIV and would not prostitute his talent by using it to exalt unworthiness, no matter what the reward. And Spinoza is but one of the unnumbered many who throughout the ages have counted something higher than money. And what is that something? It is honor.

The preservation of life itself is certainly the strongest of all man's interests, is it not? When a man is cornered, and it is a question of life or death, is there anything so powerful as his desire to live? Well, there is something which makes firemen dash into burning buildings to save sleeping children, something which has left history strewn with heroic deeds of daring sacrifice. What is that something? It is what we call a sense of honor.

Honor is so basic to life that it might almost be called the bedrock on which character is built. Without honor to undergird, love can easily become a thing of flimsy passion. It is honor which sustains the honesty of men in those dealings where the eyes of the law do not penetrate. Business places an ever greater strain on man's innate integrity. Despite the increasing regulations of business, the long-range complexity of commercial transactions leaves more loopholes through which laws can be evaded, unless one has a restraining sense of honor.

More and more indispensable, therefore, are the men of honor—men whom the law does not have to watch, men whose word is as good as their bond, men whom you can trust with your property or your loved ones, men who play the game, stand by a comrade, do the decent thing. These are the bedrock on which stable society is built.

Honor is as necessary in the realm of religion as elsewhere. Religious emotion without a sense of honor becomes weak and repulsive. The defender of the Bible who talks about keeping the Word of God inviolate but does not keep his own word; the enthusiast for missions who cries for the church to rescue the heathen, but does not stand by his own companions—such persons are deficient in honor and by that defect bring disgrace on the name of religion.

Yet a mere gentlemen's code of honor cannot save the world. For one thing, it is not inclusive enough. Codes of honor are usually limited to the groups in which they operate. The medieval knights treated the ladies of the nobility with all the courteous consideration of chivalry, but they would defile the daughters of the peasants without compunction of conscience or censure of their class. The college student often has a code of honor which distinguishes between the sisters of his classmates and the girls of the town. No, gentlemanly honor is not broad enough or inclusive enough to go out beyond class and country.

Our troubled, divided world needs something more dynamic than mere decency. We need men who are not only upright but uplifting. It is one thing to be respectable enough to obey the law; it is another thing to be godly enough to improve the law. It is good to be a gentleman who keeps his word; it is still better to care enough for truth to find out the facts and make one's word worth keeping. When honor is blended with godliness, it becomes magnetic. That's our need today.

IV

When We Are Not Enough with the World

❖❖❖❖❖❖❖❖❖❖❖

BREAKING DOWN OUR BARRIERS

If we could get a bird's-eye view of our world today, we would see it checkered and crisscrossed with walls. We would look down upon the walls of homes wherein men have enclosed their loved ones and their belongings. We would look down upon walls around factories and fences around farms. Man is a maker of walls.

Robert Frost has written a poem in which he pictures a farmer rebuilding his stone fence. The frost and weather have dislodged some of the stones. As the farmer replaces the fallen parts and contemplates the continuous care required to keep up his fences, he says to himself, "Something there is that doesn't like a wall."

How easily a wall can be formed between neighbors and friends. In my boyhood town two neighbors had a disagreement. Their houses stood on adjoining lots. The wealthier of the two decided he would not be irritated by having to look at his neighbor's living rooms, nor would he allow members of the other household to look into his windows. He built a wall high enough to shut out the view.

It was a vivid symbol of how walls can rise between friends. A word spoken, a motive misunderstood, a rumor repeated, a reconciliation refused—such are the first stones in the separating wall.

One says, "I didn't start it, and I'll not make a fool of myself trying to make up." So, standing on pride, desiring to save face, refusing to be magnanimous, neighbors build walls which divide friendships and destroy the peace of communities.

If we are to break down the personal barriers which divide individuals, we must begin with pride. No man ever choked to death swallowing his own pride. Quite the reverse. Who does not know the thrill which comes from swallowing one's resentment and making up with a friend or loved one? It is a great satisfaction to make a friend. There is even greater satisfaction in making up with a friend.

A second set of walls divides us. We fence ourselves off into social classes. We want to move in "the right set." We want to mingle with "the right people." And by "the right people" we mean not the morally righteous but the socially acceptable.

America must have no aristocracy save the aristocracy of worth and character. Washington was rich and Lincoln was poor, but who cares about that? There should be no ceiling to hold down a boy or girl with ability and character.

A third set of walls dividing us are the walls between religious groups. Religious sectarianism has been one of society's saddest sins. And yet it is born out of sincerity.

There is no cheap and easy way to remove these sectarian barriers. Saying that it doesn't matter what we believe so long as we do what is right is not the answer. It does matter what we believe, because what we believe determines what we think is right. We need strong convictions, and unless we value our own religious beliefs, we shall not have the proper respect for the beliefs of others.

When we think that on the battlefield our Jewish, Roman Catholic, and Protestant chaplains co-operate to give their ministry to men across sectarian boundaries, should not we rise above our sectarian spirit and match the comradeship of the ministers at the front?

We should be able to transform the blood, sweat, and tears of war into the brotherhood, sympathy, and tolerance of peace.

❖❖❖❖❖❖❖❖❖❖❖

LARGER LIVING

How large a world are you living in? We are all, of course, dwelling on a planet whose dimensions we know. Yet each of us is living in a world of his own size and making.

Beside you may be your own wife or husband. You may have lived together for years. Yet your worlds are not identical; and sometimes it happens that the husband and wife live in such different worlds that they have almost no common interests and hence no satisfying companionship. Or think of your son or daughter. Your own child may be dreaming and thinking way beyond you. Nobody quite knows the world of the person nearest and dearest to him.

We all, however, do know each one must live in a

world larger than himself if he is to be really alive. A certain college fraternity has this motto: "One man is no man." The Bible puts it, "None of us liveth to himself." (K.J.V.)

Some twenty-five centuries ago the prophet Isaiah saw his nation becoming a shutin. The world was pretty sick. Times were dreadfully bad, and the temptation was to draw into the shell of self-protection. In such a situation the prophet of God gave this prescription: "Enlarge the place of your tent, . . . lengthen your cords and strengthen your stakes."

And God calls us to lengthen our cords of fellowship. As a poet puts it, "Where I love, I live." We can be alive in a hundred places, though we dwell in a single room. I think of a woman in my parish. She is called a single woman, because she never married. Yet the lines of her life have gone out in all directions and to the ends of the earth.

For many years she taught a Sunday-school class. After her pupils outgrew her department, she kept in touch with them. I daresay she is now maintaining a correspondence with persons in a dozen different countries. What satisfaction these enlarging relations must bring to her advancing years! And who but God can measure the force of that web of friendliness in a world that needs so desperately to be woven together.

Also we need to strengthen our stakes in community living. As a boy on the farm my circle of acquaintances was small, but friendships were firm. My adult life has been spent in a large city. One danger of city living is that the cords of acquaintance are lengthened but the stakes of friendship are weakened.

Thackeray, I believe, once said he had many friends, but not more than a dozen whose death would spoil his appetite for breakfast. It seems a brutal remark, but it should make us think whether our lives are spreading too thin.

The United States and Canada were developed by "settlers," men and women who built themselves into community institutions, such as the homes, the churches, the schools. As our outlooks enlarge, we must not loosen our local loyalties. Trailer camps are no adequate substitute for the "settler" spirit.

When I ponder world problems in the large, I become almost despondent. Then when I turn to some small group going about its good work, or when I join with others in some local service, I take heart again. In the bosoms of our families, in the circles of our friendships, through the channels of our correspondence, we find our faith restored and our hopes quickened. Therefore, look to the lengthening of your cords of fellowship.

But if we are to lengthen our cords, safety demands we strengthen our stakes. One cannot safely enlarge his life to include even one other person without strengthening his stakes.

In the high and solemn moment of marriage, when two lives are joined "for better, for worse, for richer, for poorer, in sickness and in health, until death do us part," it is for a deep and valid reason that the vows be taken before the altar of God. Any sensible person knows that he needs higher help when he enters into life partnership with another personality, for only divine aid can preserve that union from tarnishing possessiveness, irritating friction, and petty selfishness.

As we all know, America's birth rate has greatly increased during and since the war. The cords are lengthening until we are now a nation of some 166,000,000. Such extension must be matched by deepening dedication. In national life, as in our most personal circles of home and friendship, the call is, "Lengthen your cords and strengthen your stakes."

❖❖❖❖❖❖❖❖❖❖❖❖

SALT OF THE EARTH

It is a very genuine tribute which we pay to a person when we call him "the salt of the earth." We use this expression only of those whom we know pretty well, for it is a compliment which grows out of companionship. Those whom we call "the salt of the earth" are the friends who make fellowship enjoyable, who keep the milk of human kindness flowing, who put flavor and tang into the life around them.

And this is the tribute which Jesus paid his followers. He said to them, "You are the salt of the earth."

To get the full force of the figure, let us consider the functions of salt. For one thing, salt is a subtle substance which brings out the flavor of that with which it is mixed. Salt is an element which other things, even the earth, seem to require in order to be and remain themselves. When salt is added to food in proper proportions, it does not call attention to itself but brings out the natural taste of the article seasoned. It makes the egg taste more like an egg; it makes the carrot taste more like a carrot—however desirable that may be! But when salt so dominates a dish that we become conscious of it, then it detracts. So is it with persons who are the salt of the earth. They do not call attention to themselves. They do not dominate others, but rather they help others to be more truly and richly themselves.

We should subject all our closest human relationships to the "salt" test. Are we overshadowing or enriching the personalities of those we love? I knew a girl who was radiant, able, vivacious. Now after twenty years she has become a pale copy of her dominating husband. Emerson once observed a father trying to make his son into a pattern of himself. And he rebuked the parent, saying, "You know and I know and God knows that one like you is enough for the world."

Another trait of salt is that it penetrates what it touches. It is an active agent. It is not like a sponge, absorbing what is around it, but rather it is pervasive, giving out its seasoning power. So it is with persons who are the salt of the earth. They are not mere absorbents. They do not sponge. They spread influence.

In recent years we have heard much in our search for subversive influences about "guilt by association." We say that a person is judged by the company he keeps. If one associates with sinners, he must be a sinner too. But Jesus was "a friend of sinners." The test is: Is the goodness of the good dynamic enough to redeem the badness of the bad? The sins of society will not be cleansed by lily-white aloofness, but by creative virtue which "overcomes evil with good."

Again, salt is a preservative. It checks deterioration. The forces of decay are ever at work. Our social circles have a tendency to disintegrate; our reforms are prone to run down; our enthusiasms quickly go sour. To check with all this we need those who are the salt of the earth. Jesus did not say, "You are the sugar of the earth." There is a temporary sweetness which tomorrow turns sour; but there is a saltness which keeps things sweet.

That is what the Christian's influence is to be—not a sentimentalism which sugarcoats the bitter facts of life, but a salty realism which today may not seem so pleasant but tomorrow keeps things unspoiled.

Such then, is the sweeping and forceful figure Jesus used when he said to his followers: "You are the salt of the earth." Any casual spectator looking at that little company gathered around the Galilean carpenter would surely have predicted that in a few years the little flurry would be forgotten. But nineteen centuries have passed and the salt has not lost its savor.

As a boy I saw how a little country church uplifted the moral standards of a rural community. As a young man I watched the work of the church in a county-seat town. It was the center of the social and cultural life. Even in the great city where my adult life has been lived and where the churches crouch under the eaves of the skyscrapers, religion still leavens the civic spirit.

❖❖❖❖❖❖❖❖❖❖❖

AIR-CONDITIONING OUR MINDS

Yes, we can air-condition our minds. Some months ago I was in the great state of Texas. Among other things, I enjoyed the various forms of air-conditioning down there. Hotel rooms, churches, even motor cars are air-conditioned.

My Texas friends assured me that Texas is God's own country, the best country he ever made. Hence I wondered a little why they were not satisfied with the air

59

God had made for them and wanted to make it over!
But I was glad they did, for I enjoyed their air-conditioning.

And we can condition the air of our thoughts. But we
cannot quite be trusted to do it healthily all by ourselves. We can make of our minds little ivory towers and
keep cool while things around us go to the devil. We
cannot live to ourselves like that and be content with
our own peace of mind.

We are also in danger of closing our minds to new
ideas which ought to disturb us. Closed minds are very
hard to cure, because nobody ever comes to a priest or
preacher asking to be cured of his narrow-mindedness.

Our minds may imprison us by confining us in vicious
circles of thought. Our minds keep recurring to fixed
ideas and fears. We go around in circles of frustration.
We are like the Indian who thought his blanket was too
short and cut off one end and sewed it to the other end,
making it longer.

We often think our trouble is to make both ends meet,
when our real trouble is that we are trying to make the
means of life into the ends of life.

We need higher help in air-conditioning our minds.
Often, I hear people say, "I go to the church where I get
something." That is in part a very valid reason for going.
The church should give people something to help them—
peace of mind, courage of spirit, freedom from anxiety,
even health of body.

But what so many do not go on to see, and what the
church sometimes fails to show, is that we should seek
to get something from God only that we may share it.
When we go to church to get something, we must ask
why we want it. Why do I want peace of mind? Merely
that I may be free from anxiety and smugly complacent?

60

Or that I may be a more stable and helpful member of my group? Why do I want God to give me an attractive personality? Merely that I may be admired and be successful? Or that I may add to the welfare of those who have to associate with me?

It was George Bernard Shaw, I think, who characterized some modern church congregations as a mob of hermits, each bringing his cup of self-satisfaction to be filled at church and then carrying it back to his own little cave.

The real gifts of God cannot be gotten by people who are wrapped up in their own self-interest. Ben Franklin was wise as usual when he said: "A man wrapped up in himself makes a very small bundle."

Back in World War II days, when anti-Japanese feeling ran high, Henry Sloane Coffin told a certain congregation about a church which had received a Japanese-American family into membership. After the sermon an elder of the church where Dr. Coffin was preaching came up to him and said, "If one of those little yellow beasts came to this church, he wouldn't get my vote for admission."

Dr. Coffin replied: "But remember Christ died for *them* too."

The elder answered, "Well, if he did, it wasn't worth his while."

To which Dr. Coffin quietly replied, "Were *you?*"

Some time ago I spent a night in a pleasantly air-conditioned hotel room. I left a call to be awakened. When the phone rang, the voice said: "It is seven-thirty and the temperature is 84." Shut in my room I was sheltered from the heat. But I had to go to work. And my business took me out into the heat of the day. Sooner or later we have to do business in God's world. And we had better condition ourselves to face it.

WHEN GOOD FELLOWS GET TOGETHER

A few years ago I stood on the wharf from which the Pilgrim Fathers sailed for America. It is, as you know, in the English city of Plymouth.

The day of my visit there was a bank holiday. And in the pleasure-seeking crowds surging through Plymouth's parks, I could not find many who knew much about the place from which the Pilgrims embarked. The spot is marked by a modest little arch and inscription.

I do not know whether the departure of that little company of forty-one families attracted much attention on that sixth day of September in 1620. Perhaps many were glad to see the Pilgrims go because they were dissenters from the established church. They were called "Separatists" by the English. They migrated first to Holland. And then after a few years some of them left Holland for America by way of Plymouth.

Governor William Bradford and others of their leaders referred to these twice-transplanted people as "strangers and pilgrims on the earth," using the scriptural reference in the Epistle to the Hebrews (K.J.V.). The word "pilgrim" clung to them, and by the beginning of the nineteenth century the term "Pilgrim Fathers" came into use. Thus it is striking that those who were called Separatists in England have become known to us as Pilgrim Fathers.

In the history of this little company we see revealed both the principles of separation and association. There come times in the course of human events when for the sake of conscience men have to sever old associations.

Conscientious people, like the Pilgrims, have felt constrained to cut loose from their ecclesiastical moorings and start new denominations. A situation may develop in a business organization so that a man feels obliged to leave in order to save his integrity and self-respect.

A person may join a reform movement which has noble objectives. Later subversive elements may infiltrate and change its purpose. Thereupon his duty is to withdraw lest he be deemed guilty by association.

But merely to separate from a situation or group is no adequate solution. If the English Separatists who left the Church of England had become an isolated ingrown group, they would soon have wilted away and been forgotten. But that company of Pilgrims united with other colonists and came to be known as the fathers of a new commonwealth.

Goodness can only be effective through association. You cannot really be good all by yourself. Perhaps some cynic may sarcastically say, "The only time a person can be good is when he is by himself!" But goodness cannot long exist in a vacuum.

One might cleanse his mind of all unworthy thoughts and restrain his passions from all impure desires. But would such purity be pure goodness? The Scripture reminds us that we cannot claim to love God, whom we have not seen, unless we love our fellow men, whom we do see. And can anyone be said to love his neighbor if he has no fellowship with him?

The late Sinclair Lewis once said to me something like this: "I believe in religion, but why organize it? The moment you organize religion, you kill its spontaneity." I see Mr. Lewis' point. There are times when I feel that I can come closer to God by going off to some lovely spot in the country or in the quiet of my own room than by mingling in church congregations or attending church committees. But only by organization can we effectively teach religion to our youth or use our religious faith to clean up the bad conditions of society.

Evil forces "gang up." Good forces must therefore join up. We can no more cleanse society by isolated individual effort than we can irrigate the Sahara Desert with an atomizer. If every resident of your city had a good well in his own back yard, you would not have an adequate water supply for cleaning the streets or putting out fires. There are some things we can only do together.

The subversive dangers of our day can be checked not by lone sharpshooters but by the army of the Lord. And furthermore, the high joys of our faith can be found only in fellowship.

❧❧❧❧❧❧❧❧❧❧

THE FEELING OF FELLOWSHIP

What have we in common to bind us together into fellowship?

Of course, we all share the common purpose of making the most of our own individual lives. Each of us has but one life to live on the earth. Each of us wishes to live his own life to the full. We all have pretty much the same physical appetites and the same heart hungers. As we say, human nature is much the same the world around. But while these common features show our likeness, they do not guarantee our liking one another. The fact that we hunger for the same things is often one of the causes of our competitions, jealousies, and divisions.

Another thing we have in common is the same quality

of blood. As Paul said nineteen centuries ago, "God . . . hath made of one blood all nations of men for to dwell on all the face of the earth." (K.J.V.) This fact which Paul declared to the Athenians has now been confirmed by modern biology. The blood of all races is sufficiently of the same quality that science is willing to have all our citizens, regardless of race or color, contribute to the same blood banks. But this biological fact of blood similarity has not proven powerful enough to bind men together in the bonds of brotherhood. It is one thing to recognize the need of brotherhood, it is quite another to experience the feeling of fellowship.

What gives a sense of fellowship? Isn't it what we feel when we belong to a common center of loyalty?

Take it in the family. Perhaps you recall some occasion, such as a high-school commencement, when you were put up to make a speech. The faces before you looked as uninspiring as the desert sands to a traveler dying of thirst. Your throat went dry. Your mind went blank. And then you caught sight of your parents and a sprinkling of uncles and aunts. Their friendly faces were like oases in the desert. You knew they were with you. They belonged to the same family group. They were inwardly rooting for you. You must not let them down. Yes, the family ties of blood are thicker than water.

We know, too, the fellowship we feel through loyalty to a school. If out on some South Pacific isle or in the fog of the Aleutians you run across someone from your high school or college, how strong that school bond is under such conditions.

I once heard of a letter written home by an American soldier from the Fiji Islands. He and another soldier were out walking one afternoon, when they met a couple of Fiji Islanders dressed in native costume, which was quite primitive and pretty diminutive. To the American lads the natives looked strange and wild. But when our boys stopped to make some signs to them, they were greatly surprised to discover that the Fijis spoke good English. Their surprise was heightened still further when the natives invited them to church. And then the American soldier's letter added. "And, Mother, would you believe it, they weren't cannibals, they were Methodists."

Consider the fellowship which comes from common loyalty to our country. When we meet a man on the street, the mere fact that he is an American may not arouse any particular bond of sympathy. Surrounded as we are in our home towns by fellow Americans, we take the relationship for granted. We compete among ourselves. We even quarrel among ourselves at times.

But I recall one Sunday in Mexico quite a number of years ago. In the turbulence of their election day, we were ordered to remain in our hotel to avoid the dangers which threatened on the streets. After four o'clock in the afternoon a few bullets began to fly outside our window, causing us to feel a bit homesick, to use a mild term. And then just at the height of the confusion a friendly voice from the American Embassy called to invite us to dinner on the following evening. At such a time that voice of a fellow American warmed the cockles of our hearts.

There are times when the mere fact of our citizenship and the sight of our flag stir our souls with a sense of brotherhood. It behooves us to review those common loyalties which bind us together despite the differences of wealth and color and creed.

"United we stand, divided we fall."

BETHLEHEM AND BARBED WIRE

In 1952 I fulfilled a long cherished dream. I was in the land of our Lord at the Christmas season.

My plane landed at the great, new, dynamic city of Tel Aviv. There in that vital young nation of Israel is the blending of East and West. But even more impressive to me was the meeting of the modern and the eternal.

I had stopped in the Holy Land to broadcast a Christmas message to America. Having landed in Israel, I could not go quickly across the border, which is held by the Arabs. However, I did ask to be taken as near as possible to Bethlehem. My guides drove me to a point where I could look across the brown hills to "the little town of Bethlehem."

But beside me as I watched stood a soldier with fixed bayonet. And between myself and Bethlehem stretched barbed wire marking the boundary of Israel and Jordan.

That bayonet and barbed wire were sinister reminders that the Prince of Peace, born in Bethlehem, has not yet banished war from the governments of men. But shall we give up hope? Ah, no!

Of the Babe born in Bethlehem, we might paraphrase Sir Winston Churchill's famous statement about the British airmen. We might say that in all history there is no other situation in which so many owed so much to One so little.

When a stone is dropped into a lake, it starts ripples radiating. But as the distance from where the stone fell increases, the ripples grow less and less distinct until they disappear. Not so with the Babe born in the manger at Bethlehem. The event stirred only a small ripple of excitement at the time. But as the centuries have lengthened since that time, the ripples of interest have grown into mighty waves until millions hail the birthday of Jesus as the "day of all the year the best."

Why the perennial and growing appeal of Christmas? Its beauty, its tenderness, its joy? Yes, all these are there. But a greater feature is at the center.

In Matthew's Gospel, the announcement to Joseph is that the child to be born shall be named Jesus—"For he shall save his people from their sins." (K.J.V.) And, in Luke, the angelic message to the shepherds is: "Fear not: for, behold, I bring you good tidings of great joy, which shall be to all people. For unto you is born this day in the city of David a Saviour, which is Christ the Lord." (K.J.V.)

The Bethlehem scene was realistic in its setting. The hard facts of life were there. Joseph and Mary were going up to be taxed. Taxes were just as unpleasant then as now.

The inequalities of life were there. The inn was crowded with those who could pay for it; the poor carpenter and Mary were forced to seek shelter in a stable.

The shadow of the hostile Herod was there. Danger lurked around the Babe in the manger.

Yet with all these dark features, the general impression of Bethlehem is that of goodness. Our attention is held by the mother, the loving Joseph, the humble and adoring shepherds, the reverent Wise Men. The scene turns our minds to the things that are simple, genuine, and lovely; the things that heal and build.

Christmas is not only the revelation of God, but also of man. It brings to view the divine spark of goodness in the human heart. It is the time when truth takes on its loveliest forms and speaks its simplest language; when love becomes articulate in accents which little children understand.

Christmas not only brings the world around to the

day when Christ was born, but it brings to birth the Christ-spirit in man. It reminds us that the universe is friendly and therefore restores our faith in God. It reveals that man is better than he often seems and thereby revives our faith in man.

The Babe of Bethlehem has outlived Herod and Caesar Augustus. Someday the spirit of Bethlehem will outlaw the barbed wire and the bayonet.

V

When We Are Groping

❖❖❖❖❖❖❖❖❖❖❖❖

WHEN WE ARE LOST

We dislike to lose things. A trifling loss may torment us for days. From a dropped glove or a misplaced book up to a vanished fortune or a ruined reputation, losses are distressing.

But if we were told that *we* are lost, how much would that disturb us? Of course, that would depend on the situation.

There are times when to be lost means the prospect of physical death. Admiral Richard Byrd had such an experience during his first stay in Little America as he was exploring the region around the South Pole. One night he left his cave to look at some meteorological instruments and to get some exercise. Since the danger of getting lost in that Antarctic darkness was real and also likely to be fatal, he took the precaution to set up a line of sticks in the snow to guide him. But on this particular night he walked beyond the line before he realized it. Suddenly he discovered his situation and could find no trace of a way back to his cave.

He records that there came over him a sinking, sickening sensation, and he whispered to himself, "Now you're lost." Fortunately he did find his way back before it was too late. But it is hard for us in our warm homes to imagine the full terror of being lost in polar snow with inevitable death by freezing only a few moments ahead.

There was a time when the preacher in the pulpit could stir in his hearers something of this same terrifying feeling by telling them that they were lost souls. When Jonathan Edwards in his sermons pictured sinners in the hands of an angry God on the very brink of hell, his listeners fairly rose from their seats in fear. Such "hell-fire preaching" still stirs congregations in some places, but not in many. But in our conventional churches each Sunday we pray the General Confession: "We have erred and strayed from thy ways like lost sheep."

Let us consider the lost sheep. It is not strange that sheep have served to shape so much the pattern of scriptural thought and language. Sheepherding was about the leading business of Palestine. And the shepherd's care of his sheep—patiently going after the stray one, tenderly carrying the lambs in his bosom, guarding with his body at the gate of the sheepfold during the night—all this was a fit symbol of the heavenly Father's care. It is no wonder that the Psalmist sang, "The Lord is my shepherd."

Then, too, sheep in their moods are so much like people. The lambs so lovable and so helpless, just like little children. The sheep so likable and yet so stupid, just like so many people. They go nibbling along with their noses to the ground, greedily devouring the blades of grass nearest to them, so seldom lifting their eyes to get their bearings, and thus they wander away from the flock or stray near some dangerous cliff.

Oh, it may be that the figure of the lost sheep does not seem to fit us, who think we are modern and smart. We think we know our way around pretty well. But Arthur

Holt says, "A man is lost when he cannot define his present nor plan his future."

When life has no pattern of meaning for us, it becomes almost intolerable. We may like our job so well that we never look at the clock. But we do sooner or later look at the calendar, and ask what these years are adding up to.

Where are we getting? What's the use of it all? And our pleasures; they, too, begin to pall unless the good times we have here and there are woven together into some pattern of abiding and satisfying happiness.

And if you do not think we of our day have any "lostness," listen to the words of General Omar Bradley speaking at the Tomb of the Unknown Soldier, November 11, 1948:

With the monstrous weapons man already has, humanity is in danger of being trapped by its moral adolescents. Our knowledge of science has outstripped our capacity to control it. We have too many men of science, too few of God. We have grasped the mystery of the atom and rejected the Sermon on the Mount. Man is stumbling blindly through spiritual darkness while toying with the precarious secrets of life and death. The world has achieved brilliance without wisdom, power without conscience.

Yes, whether we feel sheepish or not, we are like sheep who have gone astray following the devices and desires of our own hearts, until we have lost our sense of direction, our sense of security, our sense of real purpose.

Some years ago, King George of England sent a New Year's message to the British Commonwealth. He closed his greeting with these lines:

I said to a man who stood at the gate of the years, "Give me a light that I may tread safely into the unknown," and he replied, "Go out into the darkness and put your hand into the hand of God. That shall be to you better than a light and safer than a known way."

****

I BELIEVE

Let us start with the statement, "I believe." We may say those words in rather light vein. For instance, we say, "I believe it will rain tomorrow." That is a mere expression of opinion, a sort of guesswork. Or we may say, "I believe James Monroe was the fifth president of the United States." Here we are just stating a belief in lieu of looking up the fact.

But when we say, "I believe in God," we are going further than stating a mere guess or opinion. To believe in God means first of all to think with assent. It means that we have made up our minds that there is a God in whom we believe.

This matter of making up our minds involves more than mere intellect. Watch a little two-year-old child come into a room where several persons are standing around. The little girl looks about with her big eyes wide with wonder. Perhaps there is a pucker of puzzlement on her face as she tries to take it all in. That's what we say, isn't it, "she is taking it all in." She is taking a picture of the room, the persons, the faces. But her little mind is more than a camera registering external impressions automatically on an inner film. She is making up her mind.

The little girl spies her mother in the crowd. She believes in her mother. That is more than a belief in her mother's existence. She trusts her mother.

Similarly with grown-up observers, we look around our world. We try to take it in. We try to make up our minds about it. We see such facts as the orderliness of nature, and the fidelity of the good earth with its seasons and harvests. We see man as one who "looks before and after and pines for what is not." We see man longing for truth and beauty, for justice and mercy; and we ask whence come these ideals. If water cannot rise above its source, must there not be something at the heart of the universe which gives rise to these longings in man? We see men everywhere in all ages building altars and shrines to some Being beyond themselves. And taking it all in, we make up our minds that there must be a God to explain the factors which we see around us.

But believing in God is not just a matter of intellect. It involves the will. Some years ago I sat at the bedside of a young man who had suffered a long series of misfortunes and accidents. He said he could see no evidence of God. His trouble was that his mind was in a position analagous to his body, that is, flat on its back, waiting for God to come and prove himself. Well, God does not come and prove himself to minds flat on their backs. He comes to those who are desperately seeking him for aid to others, as he came to the sick lad's father who cried, "I believe; help thou mine unbelief." Our heavenly Father shows himself to penitent prodigals who have risen from their sins and are returning to the homeland of their innocent childhood.

As the Epistle to the Hebrews says, "Whoever would draw near to God must believe that he exists." Do you say that is begging the question? No, Paul is only telling us that in religion, as elsewhere, belief must often journey

74

ahead of factual knowledge. There were scientists who believe the atom could be split long before it was demonstrated to the rest of us.

Or consider friendship. If your friend invites you to dinner, you do not ask him for a written guarantee that there is no poison in the food. If he invites you to ride with him in his car, he does not require you to sign a waiver releasing him from damages in case of accident. If your friend bids you spend the night in his house, he does not put you under bond not to steal the valuables in the room. In short, a friend trusts himself to the fidelity of a friend.

This attitude of trust, so essential to human fellowship, is equally necessary to our relations with God. As Charles Wishart says, we must be gentlemen with God. That is, we must take some things on trust.

Do you have doubts about God? George Matheson, a young Scottish preacher, once was so beset with doubt that he wanted to give up the ministry. His friends counseled him to go on living up to the best that was in him, just as if he still believed. Matheson held on and became one of Scotland's greatest preachers.

Remember, we advance toward God feet first, rather than head first.

THE EYES OF THE HEART

Suppose you were to visit your doctor in order to have your eyes tested for glasses. He would tell you to look

75

at a wall chart on which there were lines of letters varying in size. He would ask about certain letters, "Can you see that one?" And you say, "I see." That is physical vision.

Or suppose you go to consult a lawyer about your income tax. He tries to explain the intricacies of the tax laws. After a while you say, "I see." (That might be a slight exaggeration!) To the extent that you do see the points of the law, that is mental vision.

But now suppose your young daughter comes home to dinner. She goes through the meal with what she thinks is her usual composure. She tries to keep herself under control. But you detect a suppressed emotion in your daughter. After a time you say, "Mary, out with it. I see there's something on your mind." That is more than physical or mental vision. That is seeing with the eyes of the heart.

We do not discover all the facts and values of the world unless we use the eyes of the body, the eyes of the mind, and the eyes of the heart. Paul recognizes this truth when he writes to the Ephesians. In the first chapter of his letter he tells them he is praying God to give them the spirit of wisdom and revelation. Then he uses these words: "Having the eyes of your hearts enlightened."

Pause a moment to consider how the eyes of our bodies have been enlarged and enlightened by man's inventions. By means of the telescope we have lengthened man's eyesight until we have multiplied almost to infinity the stars seen by the naked eye. With the aid of the microscope we can see a miniature world in a drop of water. By television we can penetrate stone walls and inky darkness to behold scenes long distances away.

George Orwell has awakened us with some futuristic pictures of man's ability to see into other minds. In his stark novel *1984* he sketches a world in which man will have no privacy at all. Even his most intimate thoughts in darkened rooms will be detected by devices controlled from a central bureau of dictators. It is a fanciful picture, but with enough possible realism to make it a bit terrifying.

What will the world of tomorrow become if we keep improving our mechanisms for lengthening the eyes of the body and the mind but do not have the eyes of our hearts enlightened? I do not raise the question in order to frighten us but rather to arouse us to what we are missing. God has so much more in store for us than we are now seeing.

Consider the children in our own families. We parents want them to look *up* to us, but how much time do we take really to look *at* them? Thornton Wilder, in *Our Town,* pictured a little girl returning from the land beyond the grave and saying something like this: "Mother, look at me! We never took time to look at each other when I was on earth."

And how about that life partner who has lived with us as husband or wife, sharing our joys and sorrows? Maybe we have been so taking each other for granted that we have not looked deeply into the heart. Perhaps the hair is growing gray, and strangers might think the lines in the face have marred its beauty, but when we look with the eyes of the heart, we see that love grows lovelier with the years.

And there are those persons whom we do not like. Charles Lamb, the poet, was a man of bitter prejudices. Once at a party Lamb noticed a person about whom he had written some critical words. A friend asked the poet if he did not wish to be introduced to him. "No," replied Lamb, "if I met him, I might like him."

HOW DOES GOD GUIDE US?

When we start our minds running back along the skein of events which have led our lives up to this point, we do not find in mere chance or coincidence very adequate explanations. Was it only by chance that Columbus discovered this continent? Was it merely coincidence that our founding fathers drew up the kind of Constitution which we have? Was it only the accident of birth which gave us in the crises of our history men with the characters of a Washington and a Lincoln?

It is beyond my belief that blind chance could shuffle the material elements of earth and draw from the mixture the conscience of a Socrates, the mind of a Plato, and the genius of a Shakespeare. For me the doctrine of chance does not explain the emergence of that orderliness which the physicist finds in the electron and the astronomer finds in the heavens. There seem to be purpose and plan running through creation.

In my student days a book made a deep impression on my mind. It told of the mass migration a thousand or more years ago from the Central Asia plateau of Turkestan westward until Palestine was occupied and the eastern end of the Mediterranean was closed as a trade route between Europe and India. The occupation of Palestine by "infidels" aroused the conscience of European Christians, and they launched the Crusades to free the Holy Sepulcher.

The Crusaders in crossing eastern Europe made contact with the old Greek culture, and thus was stirred a revival of learning in Europe. Vitalized by that renaissance, Europe sought to expand her trade, but because the eastern route to India was closed by the Turks, Christopher Columbus tried to find a new approach by sailing west and thus discovered America. When I trace the se-

78

quence of such events, I can hardly escape the questions of divine guidance and human destiny.

Whatever you and I may think about it, this nation was founded by men who believed that there is a higher power presiding over the human scene. Often quoted is the remark of Benjamin Franklin, one of the least pious though perhaps the most learned of our Constitution makers. When the convention seemed deadlocked by divisiveness, the aged Franklin moved to invoke divine guidance, saying: "The longer I live, the more convincing proofs I see of this truth, that God governs in the affairs of men; and if a sparrow cannot fall without His notice, is it probable that an empire can rise without His aid?"

There are various methods of guidance. The rider guides his horse by rein and whip. The shepherd guides his dog by voice and gesture. By radar we can guide the plane in the air. But when we consider the channels of communication between two personalities, we realize that there must be mutual understanding before one can effectively guide the other.

In the earliest stages of childhood, a parent has to guide the infant by the exercise of authority. The two-year-old can hardly be trusted to grasp the logic of a parent's explanation about the perils of fire and water and automobiles. Grandchildren, I am finding, are much more precocious and understanding than regular children! But even a grandchild now and then needs the guidance of authority. Nevertheless, the parent or grandparent is not content until the leading strings are superseded by the free choice of the child's own nature.

Likewise, God's guidance of his grown children is not by external coercion, but by the response of spirit to spirit.

How does God guide us? By the wisdom of the ages in books like the Bible, by the general patterns of history, by the still small voice of conscience, by the luminous insights of our best moments. Yes, and in countless other ways God shows his guiding hand to those who have eyes to see and ears to hear.

|◆◆◆◆◆◆◆◆◆◆◆◆◆|

CLINCHING OUR CONVICTIONS

When we make a decision and reach a conviction, we should do something about it. When we clinch our convictions with action, we strengthen our ideals into standards.

In common use there is quite a difference between an ideal and a standard. An ideal is something we aspire toward; a standard is something we hold ourselves to. We have lots of lofty ideals today. In fact, we have higher ideals than our grandfathers about many things, such as world peace and industrial justice. But we need to strengthen these ideals into standards of action.

When a person of high standards and decisive action appears in our midst, we feel his strength. He disposes men to follow him. Men of decision are the ones who, when a fire is raging, can calm the crowd and prevent a panic. Men of decisive action are the ones who bring order into a demoralized community and rally the forces of righteousness.

It was said of William Pitt that he formed his plans with such promptitude and executed them with such vigor that no man ever spent five minutes with him in conference without leaving a braver man than when he entered. Our moral foundations are undermined by deferring decisions and leaving our convictions unclinched by action. How pointedly Matthew's Gospel puts this truth when it reports Jesus closing the Sermon on the Mount with this statement: "Every one who hears these words of mine and does not do them will be like a foolish man who built his house upon the sand; and the rain fell and the floods came, and the winds blew and beat against that house, and it fell; and great was the fall of it." In contrast, the man who hears Christ's words and does them is like the wise man who built his house on the rock and it stood.

This day will leave each one of us either weaker or stronger. If we hear some call of duty and do nothing about it, we shall weaken the foundation of our character. If we hear the call of God to some need or service and take even one step toward it, we shall be that much the stronger. In a day which calls for positive action to replace so much prevailing negative criticism, let us, each in his own place, clinch our convictions of righteousness by some decisive deeds.

Some time ago I had trouble going to sleep—this does not often happen. I have several cures for such occasions, such as repeating scripture and quoting poetry. As a boy I learned Longfellow's "The Village Blacksmith." So I began to recite it, until I came to the lines about the old smith's work:

> Each morning sees some task begin,
>   Each evening sees it close;
> Something attempted, something done,
>   Has earned a night's repose.

As I repeated those lines, they awakened me more than ever, for they set me to thinking about the tasks I had begun and not completed. Both my desk and my conscience were far from clear!

Perhaps some of you are troubled about the things you have not finished. Some of us have so many irons in the fire, and we change them so often, that only the handles get hot. We do not go after them "hammer and tongs" like the village blacksmith and weld them into some finished object.

Maybe we lack the plodding perseverance and unflagging fortitude to see life through. Down at the Hermitage near Nashville, where Andrew Jackson lived, is a letter written by Andrew's mother when he was fourteen. That was in 1781, and his mother was going aboard a British warship at Charleston to nurse some men ill of a fever.

Fearing she might not return, his mother wrote: "Andrew, if I should not see you again, I wish you to treasure up and remember some things. In this world you will have to make your own way. To do this, you must have friends. You can make friends by being honest, keep them by being steadfast."

VI

When We Run from Responsibility

⊱✦✦✦✦✦✦✦✦⊰

FREE FOR WHAT?

Why is freedom so dear to the human heart? We of the United States in our state papers put liberty next to life itself. In listing man's inalienable rights we say, "life, liberty and the pursuit of happiness." And more than one patriotic speaker has declared that he would rather die on his feet than live on his knees.

Jesus tried to teach us that when we are freed from evils, we must go on to fill our lives with something good. He told the parable of the house which was cleansed of evil spirits and then left empty with the result that its latter state was worse than the former. Christ would set us free from *restraints* in order that he might make us free for *responsibilities*.

Here is a basic principle which we can test in any personal situation. The man who retires from business is freed from the necessity of catching the 7:58 train every morning. But most men do not enjoy retirement unless they find some new responsibilities.

The young mother is a slave to the imperious needs of her infant child. She may sometimes find those multitudinous duties very trying. If that little one is taken away by death, the mother is freed from the long hours and broken nights. But does she find such freedom satisfying? What would she not give to hear the cry of her beloved calling her to service? If she is to gain comfort and courage, she must find new commitments. Freedom from restraints is not enough. We need freedom for responsibilities.

This principle, which the early Christians had to learn, is a truth which the early Americans also had to learn. Esther Forbes in her *Life and Times of Paul Revere* tells us that after the Battle of Yorktown, which ended the fighting in the American Revolution, our soldiers were left idle. Then they grew rebellious, and for the first time there came into our vocabulary, as a word of contempt, the term "soldiering."

Did you ever stop to think of the difference in the way we use the word "soldier" in time of war and the way we use the word "soldiering" in time of peace? When war is on, the word "soldier" symbolizes energy, heroism, sacrifice. But in ordinary times, when we say a man is "soldiering on the job," we mean just the opposite of sacrifice and service. We imply that he is idly killing time.

After we had won our freedom from England in the Revolution, the tendency was to turn from being soldiers to "soldiering." It was from this dangerous drift that leaders like Washington and Jefferson and Franklin delivered us. They had to teach their countrymen to stand fast in the liberty they had won.

In the last ten years I have visited four great dictatorships—Russia, Spain, Argentina, and Yugoslavia. It is thrilling to come back from those countries to a land like ours, where we can speak without fear of secret spies, vote by secret ballots in free elections, live in houses that are exempt from search except by warrant, send our children to free public schools, and worship in churches of our own choice.

We of Canada and the United States can well thank God for our freedom. But let us not fool ourselves by thinking that freedom from dictators insures real liberty. I repeat that it is not enough to be free from restraints. We must be free for responsibilities.

In time of war we are able to make every individual feel he can do something. He can buy bonds, save gas, conserve sugar, knit socks, or do a dozen other things to aid the war effort. But when the war is over, and we ask people to work for peace, they say, "What are we to do?"

We are all familiar with the saying, "Eternal vigilance is the price of liberty." Would we preserve our freedom of thought? Then we must do some straight hard thinking. Would we insure freedom of speech? Then let us speak our convictions and support the papers which demonstrate a free press. Would we safeguard freedom of worship? Then let us keep our own churches vital and respect the convictions of others.

WHAT MAKES AMERICA?

What makes America is even more important than what America makes. The vast volume of our production may seem the basis of our prosperity. But something more than horsepower is needed for the long future.

So difficult are these days that my message springs from

a prayer. It is the prayer of Moses in one of the darkest periods of his career. In the Exodus from Egyptian slavery to the Promised Land of Canaan, the children of Israel had reached a crisis. Rebellion had arisen in their ranks.

Seemingly stalled in their advance, they turned to quarreling among themselves. Thereupon Moses, the leader, entered into a forty-day season of prayer. He prayed: "O Lord God, destroy not thy people and thine inheritance, which thou hast redeemed through thy greatness." (K.J.V.)

What is the inheritance which has made America? I read that we possess about 6 per cent of the world's land surface, 7 per cent of the world's population, and produce 50 per cent of the world's goods. Think of the difference it would have made if this continent had been poor and unproductive. Did you ever live in a community from which people were steadily moving away because it was played out? If so, you know the spirit of depression which settles on a place when all the more enterprising youth leave for greener pastures.

America has been a land where people are coming, not leaving. This has been—and is—a land of hope and opportunity.

Our founding fathers believed that God is the owner of this land of ours. We are but stewards. If we are true to our trust, we must be good stewards.

Yet wealth of material resources did not make America. Plymouth Colony and Philadelphia and Charleston were more than trading posts. If the Pilgrim Fathers had come only for gain, they would not have remained after their first year's hardships.

During that grueling first winter there was a time when the food ration was five grains of corn to each individual, when only seven healthy colonists were left to care for the sick, and when nearly one half the whole company lay in graves under the snow. Yet when the "Mayflower" returned to Europe the next spring, only the sailors were aboard.

The Pilgrims' love of liberty was cradled in religious conviction. They had been taught that every person is a child of God and thereby endowed with certain inalienable rights.

What does this country mean to us? To me it means a land where we are all equal before God and the government; not equal in ability or reward, but each good enough to have a say in determining who and what are best.

The late historian James Truslow Adams said that the greatest contribution America has made to the world is the American dream. He defined it as the dream of a land where life shall be fuller and richer with opportunity for everyone according to his ability and achievement. That dream inspired my generation. It must be preserved for our children.

╊❖❖❖❖❖❖❖❖❖❖❖╉

DUTIES AND DESIRES

Make a mental list of what you consider your duties. Alongside these, place a list of what you count your pleasures. Then see how closely they parallel. How many of our duties do we really enjoy doing?

Take, for instance, the simple matter of kindness, which is perhaps the most basic duty of human nature. Do we

always take delight in being kind, or do we often get
satisfaction in the cutting remark and the cruel little acts
of getting even? Or consider generosity, which I suppose
we would also admit to be a duty. Yet which do we enjoy
—giving as much as we can, or getting as much as we
can? Or how is it in our reading of the Bible? We who lay
claim to the name of Christian have been taught that it
is our duty to read the Holy Scripture. But the great
majority of us scarcely show that we turn to the Bible with
relish and pleasure.

Roughly speaking, there are three attitudes toward duty.
There is, first of all, the dislike of duty and the refusal
to do it. We disregard the call of conscience. We kick
over the traces of conventions, cut loose from moral obligations, and do as we like regardless of the haunting inner
voice which whispers, "You ought." But such seeming
freedom is very misleading. The gay adventurer, who
starts out dodging the strait gate and the narrow way of
disciplined duty, ends up a moral vagabond.

The second attitude toward duty is to dislike it and yet
do it. We accept certain obligations as medicine to be
taken, necessary, but unpleasant. We "grin and bear it,"
as we say, but our smile is mirthless. We drag our steps
toward duties with the unwilling air of a schoolboy who
trudges toward his classes while he sees his friends heading
for the ball field. In such a mood we may win through,
but we make the struggle a dour affair. Such a spirit of
duty-doing is responsible for the little girl's prayer: "O
Lord, make all the bad people good, and make all the
good people nice."

The third attitude toward duty is that of enjoying the
doing of it. Those who have this attitude face up to their
moral responsibilities, however exacting, and find in the
struggle the exhilaration shown by Horace Bushnell, the

great preacher of Hartford whose pulpit was a beacon light to all America. He seemed so to enjoy his Christian duties that it was said, "Even his dying was play to him." Such persons do not give the impression of being moral acrobats, tensely trying to walk the taut line of the Ten Commandments without falling off, but rather of being moral athletes, carrying their virtues with such an easy grace and surplus strength that they make goodness seem attractive to others.

It is duty done in the last fashion which is effective. Only when we enjoy doing the good deed, does our deed do much good. If a friend, who comes to stay with us in our illness, drops a hint of the pleasure he is foregoing elsewhere, he spoils the flavor of his visit. If the teacher does not enjoy her work with children, she is not likely to inspire her pupils. It is radiant goodness which gives the contagious glow.

In fact, it is only this joyous duty-doing which deserves the name of Christian. Long before Jesus, the Hebrew psalmist described the godly man as one whose "delight is in the law of the Lord." And the Master so enjoyed the performance of his duties that he forgot at times the hours of his meals. On one occasion when his disciples found him carrying on his work through the dinner hour, Jesus explained, "My meat is to do the will of him that sent me" (K.J.V.). He would rather work at what he was doing than eat.

But how can we learn to like our duties? Here are three basic rules.

First, set your will in motion toward your duty. Sometimes it takes quite a heave of will power to get going, just as a locomotive must use a spurt of power to start a train upgrade.

Second, use your imagination. As Paul said, think on

"whatever is true, whatever is honorable." The picture you paint in your mind pulls you toward it.

Third, keep practicing. The little girl may not like her finger exercises, but if she keeps on, music will get her.

It may hurt to give the first dollar, but those who give most learn that "it is more blessed to give than to receive."

❖❖❖❖❖❖❖❖❖❖❖

CONVENIENT RELIGION

If we were asked how our present American civilization is superior to former modes of living, wouldn't most of us mention physical comforts and conveniences?

Our houses are more commodious. Housekeeping has been delivered from so much of its drudgery. Hours of work are shorter. Travel is swifter.

Ours has been called a "sitting civilization." We can hear voices and music from the ends of the earth. We can fly from luncheon on the Atlantic to dinner on the Pacific. We can do and have all these things while we are seated in comfortable chairs.

Some years ago a summer camp in northern New England put out a descriptive booklet to lure patrons. It bore the intriguing title, "Roughing It Smoothly." Whatever that means, that is what we seem to want.

Do we not measure our personal advancement by the increase of our comforts? Have we not heard self-made men say, "I do not want my children to have it as hard as I had it"?

By many work is looked upon as the necessary hardship

by which we earn money to do what we want to do, and the sooner we get it over with, the better.

We are told that the church should give the people what they want. Every now and then some bright person with a flair for promotion appears to tell the churches how they can sell religion to the people.

An advertising man once analyzed the desires of people and sought to sell his findings to the churches. He listed the various popular desires in order of their appeal. I forget the exact order, but the list included such desires as: how to be happy, how to be well, how to get ahead in the world, how to get along with people. His point was that if preachers would study what people want and then fit their messages to popular desires, the churches would be full.

Well, there seems to be some logic in the argument. The church is to serve the people. It must therefore reach the people. Religion should be made winsome and attractive. Make the church as beautiful and comfortable as possible. Cushion the pews. Condition the air. Improve the music. Popularize the themes. How far we have gone in our efforts to sell religion to the people by appealing to their comfort and convenience was made vivid to me by contrast when I attended church in Russia a number of years ago.

Having been sent to the Soviet Union on a mission to learn what had happened to the relief supplies given to that country during the war, we were under the guidance of a government agency. When we asked to visit the churches, the government agents advised against it, thereby clearly showing their indifference, even their hostility, to the church. Nevertheless we insisted.

There are no cushioned pews. The worshipers stand, and the services in the Orthodox churches last three hours.

When I saw the long queues waiting to get in, the discomfort endured by those poorly dressed Russian people standing for hours, I could not help but wonder if we in this so-called Christian land take our religion as seriously as some of those Russians under a godless government.

We can carry our cult of comfort and convenience too far. A young woman came to a psychiatrist complaining that she felt lonely and left out of things. Going back into her life history the psychiatrist found that the girl had never taken any pains to be friendly. When guests came to her home, she would not go down to see them unless she was fond of them. Having never put herself out to be nice to others, she came to find herself left out.

The person who never puts himself out for a friend does not take in the joys of friendship. The person who does not put himself out for God cannot receive the blessings of religion.

The Cross cannot be made into a couch. And that church serves us the best when it helps us to serve the most.

❧❧❧❧❧❧❧❧❧❧❧

THE KREMLIN AND THE CROSS

The criticisms hurled at America by the Soviet Union and her satellites have at least one irrefutable answer. We allow our people to pick their leaders.

The Kremlin clique tries to deceive the Orient by picturing Russia as the liberator and America as the oppressor, but we are demonstrating that our rulers are not irresponsible dictators like the Politburo, but leaders answerable to the sovereign people.

When the citizens of our nation express their will through a majority vote, such a vote is called the sovereign voice of the people. Yet the sovereign people, when it inaugurates a new president or governor, requires him to take an oath or affirmation with his hand on the Bible, symbolizing that he holds his powers under the dominion of a divine authority. And when our Congress convenes to represent our people in the making of laws, its sessions are opened with prayer invoking wisdom of a divine Lawmaker.

I wonder if we Americans quite realize what it would be like to live in a land where a dictator had the last word, where there was no appeal to the general public conscience, where there was no looking up to a divine Source of right and justice. We should think about this until it sinks into our hearts.

Today the lines are drawn around the earth between two vast power blocs. One is led by the Soviet Union, which officially declares itself a godless nation. The other bloc is led by nations like the United States, Great Britain, and Canada, which call themselves Christian nations. The world is now watching to see what differences are visible in their conduct. On a world scale and before a global audience for the first time in history, this issue is being tested.

If the nations which professedly look to the Cross can demonstrate to the world that their principles and methods are superior to those of the countries led by the Kremlin, we shall open the way for a world-wide spiritual advance on a scale never before approached.

"The Son of man came not to be ministered unto, but to minister." (K.J.V.) Christ sought to rule over men in order that he might serve them. Most rulers rise to power by pretending to be the servant of the people. Even Hitler and Mussolini did that. But once in power they showed their greedy desire to dominate.

When will we learn that Christ's motive of ruling to serve is the only one which lasts? When we gain power over others for the sake of profit or domination, such rule is likely to be short-lived, as was Italy's conquest of Ethiopia and Japan's control over China. But when we use our power for service, we earn for it a welcome which grows with time.

If America now uses her strength and leadership in a genuine spirit of service, she will win the respect of the smaller nations. They will see that the Cross is better than the Kremlin.

Methods of governing as well as motives are important. Some well-intentioned persons serve others in ways which prove a disservice. A mother may earnestly desire to help her daughter, yet she may so rule her household that the girl grows up lacking in self-determination and force of character. Good parents so govern their children that the children become able to govern themselves.

A good government does not treat its people as pets or pawns. If ours is to be a government of the people and for the people, it must be a government by the people—a people concerned for their duties as well as their rights, a people responsible enough "to bear their own burdens" and responsive enough to help bear one another's burdens and so fulfill the law of Christ.

TURNING TRUANT

In my boyhood community there was to me a rather terrifying figure known as the truant officer. He was a person about whom I heard my parents talk frequently.

According to the description graven on my young mind, the truant officer had an eye sharper than an eagle and a scent keener than a bloodhound. He always got his quarry, and his quarry were bad boys who played truant from school.

Suffice it to say, I never fell into the man's clutches. However, I am not sure that my record on truancy has remained clear since boyhood.

A truant is defined as "one who stays away from business or any duty." When I look back, I fear that at many times I have deserted or avoided my place of duty.

Why does a person play truant from life's school? Sometimes because of boredom. The boy trudging to school thinks of the fishing stream or the baseball lot, and the schoolroom to him takes on the aspect of a prison.

Maybe because of irritation. The businessman, chafing under government regulations and fretted by competition, looks out the window and longs to get away.

Or it may be weariness. The young housewife, worn to the quick by the friction of petty demands, sees the glamorous existence depicted on the screen and begins to pity herself as a prisoner of routine. She is just tired of it all.

And sometimes a situation seems so hopeless that a person feels it futile to stand by any longer. For instance, the world's problems seem so baffling that many people are inclined to stop working at them. They would have America live to herself and let the world go. And many do not bother to study even our own social problems or go to the polls to vote on them.

Having seen why men play truant to their highest duties, let us consider how they do it. One way is to try to tone down the call of conscience. How plausibly we say, "Of course, we must do our duty but God meant us to use our common sense."

To be sure, we must be practical. We must use common sense. But when we tone down our ideals and dreams to what we call common sense, we may often make it so common that, as Jesus said, it is like salt which has lost its savor and is "thenceforth good for nothing, but to be cast out, and to be trodden under foot of men" (K.J.V.).

There is a saving common sense and there is a savorless common sense. Saving common sense is the product we get after we have tried what seemed at first impossible. Savorless common sense is what we think is workable and practical before we have tried the seemingly impossible.

It is the mediocre mentality which ridicules the pioneers and stones the prophets.

Or we can play truant to duty by not looking in its direction. Sometimes we avoid a moral fight which calls for our help by going down a safe side street.

Recall what Job said when he was trying to prove his moral integrity. He declared that he had made a covenant with God to rebuke him if he ever "kept quiet within doors, afraid of what the crowd would say." (Moffatt.) When a public fight is on over some moral issue, it is so pleasantly tempting just to stay quiet within doors. When a righteous cause is being ridiculed around the table, it is so comfortable to keep silent and not show our colors.

We rightly condemn the "reds" who would undermine our republic. We are suspicious of the "pinks" who are fellow travelers with the Communists. But our society is quite equally in danger from the "yellows" who have not the courage of their convictions and play truant to their duties.

But when we triumph over our truancy, we develop an inner core of self-respect and satisfaction. Moreover, we release divine resources.

A young minister of my acquaintance had a parish which did not appreciate him. He was having a hard time. A call came to a wealthy church where his type of ministry was desired. He was tempted to go. But he stayed. And then things began to break. His church rallied to him. His ministry was blessed with results.

Or I think of a woman whose husband was considered a washout. He was not good to her and he was generally "no good." She was tempted to leave him. But she kept on, hoping to find the vein of gold in him. She stuck. And she struck it. The home stood.

When we refuse to run away from duty, God runs to help us.

VII

When We Are Cheating Ourselves

❖❖❖❖❖❖❖❖❖❖❖❖

STANDING IN OUR OWN WAY

In October, 1842, Emerson entered in his Journal this sentence: "Henry Thoreau made, last night, the fine remark that as long as a man stands in his own way, everything seems to be in his way."

How true that is! One of the tragic blunders of living is to blame others for blocking our path, when in reality we are standing in our own way. We complain that competitors crowd us, or that fate is against us when the fault is within ourselves.

Sometimes we hear it said that a person is his own worst enemy. Perhaps such a statement suggests the drinker, who, with all his engaging qualities and winning ways, lacks the self-control to hold himself steady. While others are for him, he blocks his own road.

But this blunder of standing in one's own way is far broader than such cases. It is an error of all those who make life needlessly hard for themselves. It hinders a man's progress with his fellow men. It may even halt his approach to God.

For one thing, a person may be blocking the way to himself. In referring to the Prodigal Son, Jesus used the expression, "When he came to himself" (K.J.V.). Those words imply that a person is not always quite himself. We are aware of such moods at times, and there are other times when we are not ourselves without being aware of the fact.

Chesterton tells a whimsical story of an architect who was annoyed at the sight of an ugly house which he passed each day. To escape the irritating sight, he bought the house and moved into it. By living in it, he avoided looking at it. So is it with man's own nature. By living too closely within himself, a person may avoid looking at himself. He comes to take it for granted that he knows his own mind.

Or we may be standing in our own way by living too haughtily with ourselves. Stiffly proud of our own opinions, and stubbornly loyal to our past errors of judgment, we shut our eyes to the light which would reveal us to ourselves.

A schoolboy of nine, who was once explaining a picture book to his little brother of six, came across an illustration of King Charles on his way to the scaffold. "That," explained the lad, "is King Charles on his way to be blockheaded"! Well, the boy was not so far wrong. Because the monarch had been blockheaded, he was on his way to being beheaded. Thus by living too haughtily, or to narrowly, or too shortsightedly with ourselves, we block the way to our self-realization.

When we stand in our own way, we should, of course, try to get sufficiently outside of our self-confinement to see ourselves as others see us. Instead of "looking out *for* Number One," we should get off and look *at* Number One. There is a vast difference between those two viewpoints. When we are always looking out for ourselves, we seldom see ourselves because our gaze is focused on the externals around us, rather than on the resources within us. Hence, a person needs occasionally to be an outsider to himself.

Or a person may so stand in his own way that he blocks his approach to God. Prayer has been likened to a boat-hook by which the little boat is pulled to the dock. But so often we try to use prayer not as a means of drawing ourselves to God but of pulling God to ourselves.

Charles C. Merrill told of a family incident back in the Spanish-American war. A mother learned that her husband was soon to return home from the front. She wondered what her little son's reaction would be when he heard of his father's return. When she told the little fellow, he exclaimed, "I wonder what he'll bring me."

Dr. Merrill said the lad's remark made him think by contrast of Dwight L. Moody's little son. One day the great evangelist heard a knock at his study door. Being busy, he called rather brusquely, "What do you want?" He heard his little son's voice say: "I don't want anything, Daddy. I'd just like to be with you." How those words warmed Moody's heart! When we pray, let us not begin by wondering what God will bring us. Let us start by wanting to be in his company.

In certain foreign lands men have made the state their god. To the state they entrust their consciences and before its dictators they bow. What is God's rival deity in America? May it be that some of us are in danger of making ourselves into our gods? Let us remember the words of a great writer: "A man who bows down to nothing can never bear the burdens of himself."

GETTING OUR MONEY'S WORTH

Perhaps no subject has been so much discussed as the high cost of living. But what about the higher value of living, which is a more important matter than the cost?

What we get for our money is of more importance than what we pay for it. Sooner or later we pay out all we have. If I have spent $10,000 this year and saved $3,000, I may say to myself that I am ahead of this game. But when the game of life is called by the divine Umpire, all my money will be gone whether I have spent it or saved it. Hence the financial cost of living is secondary to the values received.

Let us think then about what we are getting for what we are spending. Money in itself is neither righteous nor unrighteous. But when the love of money becomes covetous greed, it becomes "the mammon of unrighteousness," for it drives men to further and further excesses.

The added curse of covetousness is that it makes men so concerned with material things that they neglect the true values of life. Just as World War II was closing, Charles Kean wrote a book in which he said, "The welfare of wealth, in one form or another, has become the dominant consideration of our contemporary order." Consider that statement. It applies to men on all economic levels. If men really put human values above money values, there would be no danger of World War III.

The only way to win the contest against the Communists is to convince the world that we are not merely seeking the welfare of possessions. Yes, and the only way to win over the worries and fears which threaten our own peace of mind is to put the welfare of personality above the welfare of our possessions.

I know we cannot completely separate the two. I realize

that property values are part of our human values. Nevertheless, we have to give one or the other the priority. That is why Jesus said, "You cannot serve God and mammon."

The Master recognized that money has its place in life. He would have his followers keep it in its place. And its proper place is as a servant of life, not a master. By being faithful in the use of money, we train ourselves for the true riches. So the Gospel says.

And now what are the true riches? They are those which do not deceive. When we go into the market to buy, we must have a sense of values or we may be taken in. Likewise in life, we must have a sense of true values or we shall "spend . . . money for that which is not bread, and . . . labor for that which does not satisfy."

True riches stand the test of time. They give us as much satisfaction after they have been gotten as they promised to give when we were pursuing them. They do not tarnish by use nor worry their possessors by fear of loss.

True riches make a man worth more than the estate which he leaves. "What was he worth?" we ask when a man's will is probated. The answer is usually given in terms of money.

The true answer is in terms of service. What was he worth to the world? Whom did he help? What lives did he enrich? In the Hall of Fame of Famous Americans there have now been placed some eighty busts of our nation's greatest. Not one of them was chosen merely for his monetary wealth. They were selected for the significance of their contribution to society.

"You Can't Take It with You" was the title of a long-run Broadway play. It pointed the futility of feverishly living for the things which must be left behind at death. But true riches are those which so enter into the enrichment of character that when the spirit leaves its temple of clay they can be taken along.

Yes, the cost of living is high. But there can be a *value* of living which is worth more than it costs.

THE ART OF OWNING

The Master of life appeared utterly indifferent to money for his own use. There is no mention of what Jesus earned as a carpenter, of what he received as a teacher, of what he spent as a traveler. Jesus is never recorded as asking for alms, and the Gospels contain no treasurer's report.

But while Jesus seemed free from any personal concern about money, there is scarcely any subject to which he made more frequent reference. Realist that he was, he recognized how the considerations of wealth are woven into the warp and woof of everyday living. He lived in an atmosphere charged with materialism. This accounts for the frequency of his lightning flashes on the subject of money.

He saw that the love of money had developed an almost demonic power which he called "mammon." He saw this love of money, this mammon, as the very rival of God. He declared, "No man can serve two masters: for either he will hate the one, and love the other; or else he will hold to the one, and despise the other." (K.J.V.)

In the light of Jesus' teachings, we cannot simply say that he bade his followers sever themselves from all possessions. In his parables Jesus seems to recognize the right of private property. For instance, in his parable of the invitations to the great supper, he cited the excuses given by certain guests. One said, "I have bought a piece of ground, and I must needs go and see it." (K.J.V.) Another said, "I have bought five yoke of oxen, and I go to prove them." Jesus condemned the making of such excuses, but he did not raise the issue of the right to own the field and the oxen.

Apparently recognizing the right to own property, he sought to teach the *right* way of owning it. Everyone owns something. Even Communism has not gone so far as to encourage community toothbrushes! The relation of religion to business has to be considered, for business without religion becomes sordid, and religion without business becomes sentimentally divorced from daily living. Jesus would teach us how to live in a world of things, owning our rightful share without being possessed by them.

And in learning the art of owning, I think Jesus would have us first consider the source of what we possess. The art of owning begins in the grace of gratitude. The thoughtful person sees that his possessions derive from sources beyond his efforts. "The earth is the Lord's and the fullness thereof." The British recognized their indebtedness to God by carving that sentence on the Bank of England. From the Creator comes the strength of body and the power of thought which enable us to use the bounties of earth.

Consider one of the most seemingly self-created acts we can imagine—a pianist playing his own composition. The theme is his own. The skill of hand is his own. But who gave him that brain to dream, that heart to feel, that hand to play? Parents and teachers were involved in the preparation of these. And back of these is the genius which is the gift of the Creator. And as for the instrument on which he is playing, who can easily compute the lands from which its materials are drawn, the workmen engaged in the making and transporting of them?

We would be happier if we thought more about the contributions of others to us and less about the competition of others with us.

And along with the source of our possessions, we should think of their *value*. William Jennings Bryan once asked a lyceum audience the question, "How much can a man honestly earn in a lifetime?" He suggested an answer to his own question. "$100,000." Remember this was more than forty years ago. Allowing $3,000 a year as an average wage and thirty years as a normal working period, a man would earn bout $100,000 in his lifetime.

Then Mr. Bryan went on to ask, "Could a man honestly earn a million dollars?" "Yes," he said, "he could." "Could he honestly earn ten million dollars?" "Yes," rhetorically answered Mr. Bryan, "for who could estimate what a man like Edison or Lincoln or Pasteur was worth to the world?" Then he quickly added, "But those men were so busy earning those values that they did not bother much about collecting the rewards for them."

It is values, not price marks, which make the art of owning.

IF WE COULD NOT GIVE AT ALL

From infancy we were reared by those who gave of themselves for us—mothers who spent sleepless nights worrying about us, and fathers who worked hard to provide for us. Our birthdays were gladdened by presents. The schooling we received was a service beyond what we paid for. The protection of our laws, the freedom of our land, the enriching friendships along the way—all these are gifts. Only by the grace of givers are we alive today.

Now take this in reverse. Suppose we never had a chance to give to anyone. Suppose we could never give to our children, never see their eyes dance with joy at something we do for them. Suppose you saw a little child struck down in front of your house by a passing truck. He was badly hurt—and you could not give any aid whatsoever.

A friend of mine had an only child who was killed in a motor accident a few years ago. She left a little daughter who is being cared for by her father and his family. My friend, the grandfather, is never allowed to see her or to do anything for her. His heart is full to bursting as he yearns to give but is frustrated.

I know how many appeals we get and how we become irritated by them. But suppose we were never asked to give at all. A man once prominent in a Pennsylvania city lost his position and property. He had been a leader in his community. He drifted into New York and took lodgings, looking for a job. He said to me: "Once I was besieged by phone calls to the point of distraction. But now the phone never rings. The lonely silence is unbearable."

Mothers are worn to the edge of patience by little tots

who tug at them and try to pull them toward counters to buy things they do not need and cannot afford. But what mother would not rather feel the pull of those provoking little toddlers than to look into the eyes of her child lying too sick to ask for anything or to be tempted by any toy?

Never to receive anything—that would be fatal, for we cannot live without what others give to us. But never to give anything—that also would be fatal.

The Master saw those who defeated themselves by thinking only of getting, those who lived pinched lives by pinching their pennies. He told the story of the rich farmer who thought only of building larger barns to house his bountiful crops and then died in the night.

In contrast to such niggardly people Jesus was drawn to those generous persons like the poor widow who put into the temple treasury all she had; and the grateful woman who, not counting the cost, poured the precious perfume on his head and feet. Paul said, "God loveth a cheerful giver." (K.J.V.) And can we not see why? Because a cheerful giver is a lovable character. We all love generous magnanimous givers.

When Jesus, therefore, bade people to give, he was not a beggar. He was a life-begetter. And when worthy causes today ask you to give, do not think of them begging merely for their own interests. They are really begetters of life. They are opening the channels to bigger, better, more joyous living. It is through giving that we fulfill our selfhood.

A few years ago I stood in the American Embassy at Moscow looking across at the Kremlin. An officer of the embassy who stood beside me said, "I do not believe the word charity is still in the Soviet vocabulary. They have ceased to understand the word." He was explaining why the Russians misunderstood and maligned American programs of giving, such as the Marshall Plan. They thought that anyone who gave must have some ax to grind.

Let us admit that giving is sometimes tainted with self-interest. Let us recognize also that self-respecting persons want justice rather than charity. Nevertheless, we cannot run society on the basis of cold justice. Nor can government do by taxation all that individuals can do by personal generosity. Increased taxes must not be allowed to dry up the milk of human kindness.

The Master of life said, "It is more blessed to give than to receive." (K.J.V.) Why? You can discover the secret this very day.

❧❧❧❧❧❧❧❧❧❧❧❧

PRIDE OF SELF-SUFFICIENCY

No doubt all of us are familiar with the expression "the handwriting on the wall." It has a sobering sound. When we say a person has seen "the handwriting on the wall," we mean he has seen the sign of divine judgment on what he is doing. It implies the beginning of the end.

We may not all know the origin of it in the story of Belshazzar's feast. Belshazzar was the son of Nebuchadnezzar, the powerful Babylonian king who, in the sixth century before Christ, captured Jerusalem and carried away many hostages and much treasure. Nebuchadnezzar attained such power that the Eastern World trembled at his step. But his later years were pathetic. His power slipped; he became senile; and his end was inglorious.

Belshazzar, his son, learned nothing from his father's fall. His own head was turned with vanity when he ascended the royal throne. One day he made a great feast for his courtiers. Drunk with power, he ordered to have brought the sacred vessels which his father, Nebuchadnezzar, had carried away from the temple at Jerusalem. From these temple vessels he and his riotous party drank freely and further debauched themselves.

Then the record in the book of Daniel is that there appeared handwriting on the wall. The king became frightened and summoned his soothsayers to interpret the writing. When they were unable to translate it, Daniel was called. Among the words which he saw there was this sentence: "You have been weighed in the balances and art found wanting."

Consider the verdict pronounced on Belshazzar. That verdict was based on three charges in the indictment which Daniel brought against the king. I shall deal with only one of them.

The first charge was this: Belshazzar had not humbled himself before the Lord. He had seen the fate of his father, but he had not learned humility. He was guilty of the pride of self-sufficiency.

In listing the seven deadly sins the church fathers put pride first. At first we may be inclined to wonder at this, for pride is not "a monster of such frightful mien, as to be hated needs but to be seen." Pride is not a vicious sin like murder, or a shabby sin like lust. It does not look very deadly, and therein lies part of its deadliness.

It is the poisonous combination of some quite wholesome qualities. We encourage pride in one's work as a spur to achievement. We encourage belief in oneself as a cure for inferiority. We encourage self-reliance as a recipe for independence and individual enterprise. Then, alas, these good traits can so easily be perverted into a self-sufficiency which deadens the nerve that detects sin and hardens the arteries that feed virtue. Pride may begin as a wholesome stimulant and then go on to become a deadly drug.

The very virtues which make for material progress become the pride of self-sufficiency, until men think they can get along without God. And when a nation tries to get along without God, it gets a dictator. And this pride of self-sufficiency pervades all modern culture. We count ourselves so clever, we do not feel the need of God. Dazzled by man's inventions, riding on man-made trains, driving man-made cars, counting on man's political science to solve our social ills and on man's medical science to cure our bodily pains—we feel no daily dependence on God.

Our forefathers lived closer to the soil. They were directly dependent on God's rain, God's sun, God's good earth. They planted; God gave the increase. Yes, the machine age with all the blessings it has brought, has lessened our sense of dependence on God, and thereby has encouraged the pride of self-sufficiency.

Such pride can be broken by the "shock treatment." Danger or disaster can shake us out of our self-sufficiency. In the spring of 1940 when Hitler was at the gates of France, Parisians flocked to prayer. But why wait for crashes to bring us to our knees?

Daily self-examination, love, and prayer will help to keep us from the pride of self-sufficiency.

NATURE'S FIRST LAW

Firmly embedded in the mind of the race is the old maxim, "Self-preservation is nature's first law." When a person is driven down to the rock-bottom decisions of life and death, he will struggle to the last ditch in order to save himself. The man on the street will tell you that each fellow is looking out for Number One.

Of course, he may tell you there are exceptions. A devoted mother will die for her child. A husband will often give his life for his wife. A true officer will perish at his post to save his ship. But are not such heroic emergencies only the exceptions which prove the rule?

There is a note of falseness in a person's going around asserting his willingness to die for others. The husband, for instance, who goes about telling his wife he would gladly die for her is quite often one who does not work very sacrificially for her. And the patriot who in Fourth of July orations and political campaigns shouts his determination to give his life for his beloved land is frequently one who so takes advantage of his government that we almost wish he would go out and die for it.

We feel disposed to label such language as "heroics." We suspect its genuineness. Jesus, himself, seemed so to regard it. The Master saw through all shallow sentimentalism. He based his program on the bedrock elements of human nature.

He began his service to men on the principle of self-preservation as nature's first law. He came to people who were being crushed and cramped by hard conditions and social injustice. He knew that his countrymen desired to save themselves and to secure a larger life. His first announced purpose was to help them in this self-preservation.

His first sermon in his home town of Nazareth was a proclamation that his purpose was to give health, liberty, and life. When he finished making this announcement, he turned to his hearers and said, "Ye will surely say unto me this proverb, Physician, heal thyself" (K.J.V.) .

Yes, that is exactly what we do say to anyone who comes offering us health or help. We naturally assume that if a person has found a blessing or cure of any kind, he will help himself with it. And we are skeptical of any solution which does not appear to have worked in the case of him who offers it.

One night on a street corner I saw a long-haired quack selling success pamphlets which were supposed to guarantee the way to health and prosperity. As I looked at his frayed sleeves I felt like saying, "Physician, heal thyself." It made me think of the friend who told me that he knew what were the sure things to buy on the stock market, but before he left he asked for a loan.

Yet the Great Physician pointed out the paradox in this law of self-preservation. There is a deeper sense in which we save ourselves by losing ourselves. The fellow who is always looking out for Number One does not really see Number One. We must lose sight of ourselves in order to find our real selves.

The person who thinks too much about his own health becomes a miser of his strength and makes himself miserable watching for germs and ailments. I know a fellow who is anxious about everything he eats and does, asking whether it is good for him. How much better he would be if he forgot himself in finding what he is good for.

We do not preserve the strength of our bodies by protecting them from work, but by using our muscles. We do not save the health of our minds by sheltering them from study but by straight, hard thinking.

We do not secure our happiness by looking first to our own interests but by looking out in love for the welfare of others. Therefore, when his neighbors said to Jesus, "Physician, heal thyself," he answered by citing Hebrew prophets who had gone forth to help others even in other places and among other peoples.

Self-preservation, yes. But remember, we save love by spending it. And there are even times when we save our souls by losing our bodies

VIII

When We Are Missing Too Much

❖❖❖❖❖❖❖❖❖❖❖❖

OUR BIRTHRIGHT

What does the word birthright mean to us? The definition I read is: "Right by birth; a privilege or possession into which one is born."

And what rights do we have at birth? Hearing so many clamoring for their rights without giving thought to their duties, some persons I know feel inclined to the view that rights are only privileges conferred by society on those who earn them. And certainly we cannot stress strongly enough the truth that rights involve duties and obligations.

Nevertheless, can we deny that there are certain divine rights which are ours at birth? The child is born into the world not by his own request. God and the parents who co-operate with him in creating the child are responsible for its coming. Less than human would be the parents who, having brought a child into the world, did not feel concerned to take care of him during his helplessness.

And Jesus pictured God as a heavenly Father more eager than earthly parents to give good things to his children. Therefore, natural instinct, confirmed and heightened by

Christian teaching, makes us respond to the rightful claim of children for the care necessary to launch them out of the harbor of infancy into the stream of life where they can sail under their own power. Thus every child has a birthright.

The world does not owe every child a living, but it does owe him access to the things by which life can be lived. That is the child's birthright. Some forty years ago Richard Cabot wrote a book in which he listed four things as the factors by which men live.

The first is work. When the author says work is one of the things men live by, he does not mean merely that we have to work to support ourselves. He is saying rather that without work we do not really live. We live to work even more truly than we work to live. Human energies turn in on themselves destructively if they have nothing to work on. One of my most interesting friends is a man of leisure, who probably has never held a paid position in his life. But he is not content to be idle and useless. He is ever helping his friends, looking up useful information, doing unusual things. The desire to be of use, to find one's place in the world's economy, is a part of our native endowment; and the person who is denied it is being deprived of part of his birthright.

The second thing by which we live is play. The right to play is part of a child's birthright. The child who has no place to play is being deprived of his God-given right. The child who has no one to play with is being stunted in his development. The child with no guidance in play will likely fall into habits of willfulness and wastefulness which will handicap his future.

And now along with work and play, there is a third thing men live by. That is love. We are made for love, and without it we are deprived of our birthright. It is

hard to imagine a child born into a home which denies
it love. Try to imagine a little girl smiling up into her
mother's face only to be met with a cold stare. Try to
imagine a little fellow reaching out his arms trustingly to
a father who turns away and lets him fall. To be loved is
part of a child's birthright.

The fourth and last of the things men live by is worship. We cannot put the whole of ourselves into our work
and our play and our love. A child has a right to that
larger fellowship with God. A child takes to religion
naturally, and to coop him up in a little earthly cage of
material things is to clip his wings.

I know a little girl who goes each Sunday morning to
Sunday school. She calls it "sunny school." As her grandfather, of course I think she helps make it a "sunny
school." And religion, when properly taught, serves to
furnish the sunshine for healthy growth.

One of our most discussed questions is whether religion
can be taught in our public schools. Certainly we must
keep public education free from any sectarian influence.
But surely our three great faiths, Protestant, Roman Catholic, and Jewish can agree on some basic fundamentals.

Our social welfare rests on moral and spiritual values.
These belong to our children's birthright.

GROWING UP

In our national budget the biggest bulk of money goes
for military defense. But next to the billions spent for

defense, the largest amount which Americans spend for public service is for education.

We want our children to grow up mentally and physically. At times parents have moods when they wish they could keep their children in the childhood stage of unfolding surprise and unstudied charm, but this parental feeling is not nearly so deep as the desire to see the child develop.

In a certain house out in Knox County, Ohio, there is a doorway which shows marks registering the growth of a boy. On his birthdays that boy would stand up against the doorjamb, make himself as tall as he could, and his father would mark the height. The proud father would stretch his son to measure his gain in height and then almost stretch the truth to prove to his friends how much above average his offspring was.

Yes, we all want to grow up. And what sadness is caused by failure to grow. When physical growth is arrested, leaving a stunted body, it is a near tragedy. And when the development of the mind stops and the body goes on growing, the result is still more pathetic.

There are other forms of arrested development not so outwardly apparent which may have very serious social consequences. Think what devastation Adolph Hitler wrought because his emotional development was somehow twisted.

A mother, exasperated by the tantrums of an eight-year-old, cried, "Don't be a baby!" And another mother in a restaurant so lost her temper and poise over some trivial discomfiture that her daughter, home from school, blushed and was heard to say, "Mother, act your age."

How numerous are the examples of arrested development—the boy who won't play unless he can run the show; the woman who sulks when she cannot have her own way; the man of forty who, finding himself thwarted in something, takes it out by storming around the office or browbeating his wife.

Growing up is a growing-out-of. We outgrow our childhood clothes and playthings. As Paul said, "When I became a man, I put away childish things." (K.J.V.) And that should mean our childishness.

Babies are born self-centered. The infant is the center of attention and desires. He wants what he wants when he wants it. If a child's desires are not trained and trimmed, his childishness expands, but he does not grow up. The result is like that of the disillusioned young fellow who followed his self-indulgence until he sadly said, "I took what I wanted until I no longer wanted what I took."

In a good home a child's selfishness is soon tempered by environment. The father's guiding hand, the mother's all-encompassing love, the living together—all combine to make the child aware that he belongs to a group. Then the little self expands to include the interests of others, so that what hurts sister Mary hurts brother John; and when one member of the family wins an honor, all rejoice.

Growing up is a growing-into as well as a growing-out-of. The boy goes to school and grows up into the interests of the school. When he finishes school, he settles in a community. And if he is a good citizen, he grows up into the activities and responsibilities of the community. Then if he is patriotic enough to be worthy of the land which protects him, he grows up into the interests of his nation, and is concerned for its welfare.

If he is godly enough, he grows up into the interests of the whole family of God throughout the world.

The man who grows *up and into* will never be *down and out*.

THE DANGEROUS AGE

What is life's most dangerous age? In a group of press representatives and church leaders the question was raised as to what could be done to prepare America against the spiritual perils of the hour.

Several of those present swung the point of the issue back to the children. Childhood, they maintained, is the key to curing our social ills. Train a child in the way he should go, and he will not depart from it. Certainly childhood is the most plastic age, and the perils which threaten early youth can hardly be exaggerated. Nevertheless, I do not believe childhood is life's most dangerous age.

If not childhood, then perhaps life's most dangerous age is the adolescent period, when the budding powers of personality are branching out in all directions, or the years following when youth are leaving home for college or for work. Certainly that formative time when sons and daughters leave the safeguards of parental guidance is a period fraught with momentous risks and dangers. Yet I hardly believe that is life's most perilous period.

The conviction has deepened upon me that life's most dangerous period is middle age. It is those in their middle years who find their youthful goals still so far from attainment, those for whom the race has slowed down from a run to a walk, or perhaps those who feel the temptation to loosen the yoke of Christ and let down the standards. It seems justifiable to apply to life the words of the psalmist and say there is a "destruction that wasteth at noonday" (K.J.V.).

The inability to carry the ideals and expectations of youth through middle age without breaking is one of life's most common phenomena. Insurance actuaries tell us how amazingly few of the young men who are running merrily at twenty-five pass the sixty-fifth milestone with financial colors flying. And the failure of financial hopes is only one of the minor casualties of maturity.

Do not misunderstand me. I am not minimizing the need of safeguarding the young. The work of the Boy Scouts, the Girl Scouts, the Y.M.C.A. and the Y.W.C.A. cannot be too highly praised as defenders of youth. I know how large a proportion of our criminals are young. Flagrant crimes occur with such tragic frequency in youth.

The sins of middle age, on the other hand, are often sins of the mind. They are more subtle. They do not always land their perpetrators behind bars or even in disgrace. Therein lies part of their added peril. Was that not why our Lord put such emphasis on the sins of the mind, like pride, selfishness, and greed, rather than on drunkenness, murder, theft, and the like? These latter flagrant sins breed their own resistance through the disgrace they entail. But the sins of the mind and spirit can go on doing their devilish work without loss of respectability.

Moreover, the sins of middle age are more socially destructive because by that time men are in places of power. Waywardness at the wheel of a high-powered motor is more dangerous than waywardness on a lad's tricycle. A selfish corrupt person in a place of authority can do more damage than a dozen drunken derelicts.

Also, in maturity we are inclined to be so smugly self-assured. Just when we feel safest, just when we are surest of ourselves, that is the time we most need to watch. And who is watching over us in middle age? When I meet the schoolteachers of America, I am heartened by the thought of what good care youth is receiving. But we grownups have to be our own guardians.

It is in the mind that the dangers of middle age often show themselves. It may be a hardening of the arteries of thought which causes a loss of open-mindedness, a toughening of opinion into prejudice, preventing the flow of new ideas and the fair facing of unpleasant truths. When Christ confronted the men whose mental arteries had hardened, he set a little child in their midst and said, "Unless you turn and become like children, you will never enter the kingdom of heaven." Have we lost that open-mindedness and open-heartedness of childhood?

Get out an old photograph of yourself at twelve or sixteen or eighteen. Look into your own youthful eyes and ask yourself some questions like these: Have I lost some of my dreams? Are my ideals higher or lower? Are my tastes getting more wholesome or more artificial? Do I wink at wrongs which used to shock me? Am I as much of a man as my mother expected me to be?

USING OUR GAINS

In the twelfth chapter of Proverbs is this bit of wisdom: "The slothful man roasteth not that which he took in hunting: but the substance of a diligent man is precious." (K.J.V.)

This homely proverb calls to my mind a hunting camp. Most men are fond of hunting. In fact there is such a thrill in the chase that even a lazy man likes to hunt. But the dressing and roasting of the animals caught are not so engaging. Hence, some sportsmen, having made their kill or catch, leave the drudgery to the paid guides. The zest of the chase ends with the catching. That is the truth of the old proverb, "The slothful man roasteth not that which he took in hunting."

This principle may be seen in almost every sphere of living. We are better at hunting than we are in developing what we catch.

Take it in the matter of health. What eager hunters of health we are. What time and travel we spend in seeking out climates and cures which will add to our physical powers. But how fully do we use these physical senses for whose health we are so concerned?

Contrast the full rich life enjoyed by the crippled slave Epictetus with the meager satisfactions that some of us get out of our ample modern environment with our healthy senses.

Or when I compare how much Helen Keller gets through her three senses with what I do with my five healthy ones, she seems to me like the artist Paganini making exquisite melody on one or two remaining strings of a damaged violin, while I seem like a village trap drummer surrounded by all sorts of instruments which I hit only occasionally. When we think how much life we miss with our healthy senses, we merit Jesus' rebuking question, "Having eyes, see ye not? and having ears, hear ye not?" (K.J.V.)

Or turn to the realm of our material possessions. There is a thrill in acquiring possession of beautiful properties, in building a home, in collecting books or art. But we do not really own a thing when we have put the label of property ownership upon it. We spiritually possess it only when it becomes food for our minds and souls.

An American statesman tells of visiting Hermann Goering in 1940 at that colossal place which the latter had built outside of Berlin. Goering had collected treasures from all the plundered corners of Europe. Specimens of finest art stood alongside the cheapest chromos. The vulgarity of the place and the lack of discrimination showed that the owner did not appreciate the value of what he had collected.

We may adorn our walls with exquisite pictures and line our shelves with rare editions, but it is the books and art we mentally devour which enrich our souls. And many are the hunters of wealth and art who do not roast that which they take in hunting.

Or carry our proverb over into the realm of invention and discovery. Man with his God-given endowments of curiosity and creativity is ever dazzling the world with new inventions. When I think of the amazing wonders of TV and radio, I remember what Henry Thoreau cynically said when he learned of the laying of the Atlantic cable. Thoreau's caustic comment was, "Yes, it's wonderful, but probably the first news that comes over will be that Princess Adelaide has the whooping cough."

Alas, our means of communication do sometimes seem to improve faster than what we have to say over them. We perfect our devices but we do not develop them to furnish food for our souls.

Or turn to the sphere of friendship and family ties. We speak of winning a friend or winning a wife. And truly to go out and capture the heart of another is just about the most exciting and satisfying game there is. And yet how we fail to develop the friends we have in our ambition to enlarge our social circles. And, alas, how many wreck the romance of their first love in their restless chase after new thrills!

We Americans talk about our freedoms. Think how much blood was shed to win for us the right to vote. Yet scarcely more than half of our citizens take the trouble to cast the ballots for which our fathers bled. And more than a majority of us do not exert ourselves to enter once a week the churches which our ancestors died to keep open.

Some years ago I spent a night in Nazareth. I thought what a primitive place it would be to stay in for a month. Yet Jesus lived there for thirty years and made his the richest life the world has ever known. He made so much out of so little. We make so little out of so much.

❖❖❖❖❖❖❖❖❖❖❖

HELPING THE STRONG

So much has been written and done about the weak that I want to ask what are we doing for the strong— those who feel no need of a physician. Certainly good strategy demands that we save the strong.

Educators are recognizing that the school makes a mistake when it gears its program to the dullest pupils and neglects the development of the brightest. A society weakens itself when it ignores the cultivation of its sturdiest stock in its emphasis on the rescue of the subnormal and the weaklings. The church, likewise, exists not merely as a hospital to mend broken lives and cure sick souls. It is also a vast public health service to prevent moral disease and preserve the well-being of the strong.

If we are seeking to further the kingdom of God, we must save the strong as well as the weak.

Consider, therefore, what, if anything, the Great Physician can do for those who feel no particular need of his services. First of all, he can awaken the strong to what they are missing. One mark of a vital person is that he does not want to miss anything. He wishes to be in on what is going on.

The restlessness of our time reveals the fear that we are missing something. Multitudes of us are tormented by the thought that we are not getting as much out of life as we ought. We see our youth passing into age with many of their hopes unfulfilled. We struggle for the prizes of business or profession, but even when we attain them, we look wistfully beyond for something more. We set forth into a world of pleasure in order to "see life" as we say, and many are only made cynical thereby. We look forward to the romance of marriage and too tragically often that leaves a sense of something lacking.

Yet in all this restlessness we so rarely turn to the Great Physician to find out what we are missing. Certainly the Man of Nazareth had something which our restless people are missing, however strong they feel. We may be healthy go-getters, but are we getting as much out of life as he did? He had no property, not even a home, yet rich young men consulted him to learn his secret. He made so much out of so little. Can we afford to miss what he got?

Strength is a deceitful thing. In the matter of physical health, a thoughtful person realizes that he cannot always trust his feelings as accurate. Our most serious diseases may start without pain. And in our spiritual natures it is even more easy to be deceived. How often it happens that a person is weakest at the point where he thinks himself

125

strongest. Our good traits of character are much like the grain in wood. It is the grain which gives wood its beauty, but if you wish to split it, just hit it along the grain. Similarly, it is along the grain of his good traits that a man's character is most easily cracked open.

We feel so sure of our strong points that we leave them unguarded. Or we become proud of them, and pride makes a good trait bad. Let a man become too proud of his purity, and he becomes priggish and prudish. Let a person pride himself on his strong convictions, and if he is not careful they will turn into intolerance. There is a lot of stupid stubbornness strutting around under the guise of strong-mindedness. Strength is almost as deceitful as insanity.

America's industrial power is still the marvel of the world. Listen to this tribute. Back in 1943 when the war was passing its turning point, a leader in Europe said: "Without the miracle of America's production, the United Nations could not possibly have hoped to win." The leader who said that was Joseph Stalin.

When I compare our factories with those I saw in Russia a few years ago, I realize how far we surpass our Soviet rival. But we dare not rest on our laurels. The basic strength of America is not in her factories but in her faith. Our character must be the stronger—enough to control our strength.

In the game of life the winner often becomes intoxicated with his own success. Of King Uzziah it was written: "His name spread far abroad; for he was marvellously helped, till he was strong. But when he was strong, his heart was lifted up to his destruction." (K.J.V.) We need God in our strength as truly as in our weakness.

SHARING OUR INTERESTS

Two young men attended the same school. They were drawn to each other by mutual attraction. They had many of the same interests. They were so mentally in tune that they could share each other's thoughts often without words.

They graduated and they married. One threw himself into work with the underprivileged. The other entered the area of business. Their lines of thinking began to diverge. Being immersed in their own tasks and giving themselves to different problems, they saw each other less frequently and ceased to share thoughts and pleasures. When they did meet they talked about surface matters, never getting down to the old deep confidences. Thus they grew apart, each feeling the other no longer cared.

At a recent meeting they talked over old times. The frozen springs of their hearts began to flow. One of them put in a letter afterwards what he would have found it hard to say face to face. He wrote: "All these intervening separated years seemed to fade away. The old affection abides."

This may not seem a very exciting case of estrangement and reconciliation, but to the persons involved there came feelings too deep for words.

As in the realms of friendship, so also in the home hearts can become estranged. Lack of attention can take luster from the romance of early marriage. The rush of modern living and the specialization of modern work often lessen the periods of shared thinking and playing.

When husband and wife do not share each other's thoughts, each can frequently read something into the thinking of the other. Meaningless or unintentional acts may start suspicions. Love may cease to advance and hearts go on the defensive. Estrangement starts and all too often does not stop short of actual separation.

Also we children of God can become estranged from our heavenly Father. This may happen in various ways, sometimes through neglect. Just as friendship has to be cultivated if it is to be kept vital, so friendship with God fades if neglected.

If the child lives in an environment where God is not spoken of, he ceases to think about God. God becomes an unreal Stranger, a Being of whom he hears only when he has done wrong, and then only as One who will punish him. Thus in the child's thinking God changes from a Friend, a very present help in time of trouble, to a sort of policeman whom he avoids.

Another way of becoming estranged from God is through resentment. This may take shape of bitterness against life and its conditions. The idea that God is responsible for whatever happens to us sometimes leads men to think of God as the cause of their trouble.

Not many men grow so bitter that they shake their fists in the face of God, but they think of life as a battle and God as an unfair Umpire. They become estranged through hardness and resentment.

We cannot be happy in estrangement, either from earthly friends or from our heavenly Father, because our hearts are made to love. They can feel at home only in the atmosphere of love.

John Howard Payne is believed to have written "Home, Sweet Home" in the Palais Royale at Paris. In his day that was the center of glamorous restaurants and entertainment. But "be it ever so humble, there's no place like home," where there are those for whom we care and those who care for us.

And our earthly homes need to be set in an eternal at-homeness. That is why the psalmist looked to God and said, "Thou hast been our dwelling place in all generations." The psalmist was singing a larger version of "Home, Sweet Home."

IX

When We Need a Manager

‣◈‣◈‣◈‣◈‣◈‣◈◆

WHAT IS TIME?

If we were asked, "What is the time?" we would consult our watches and answer quickly. But if we were asked, "What is time?" how would we answer? There is a mystery about time which has ever fascinated the world's best thinkers.

We talk about time in common daily terms. We speak of "making time," of "saving time," of "spending time," of "killing time." We all know what we mean by such expressions. What is time?

We say, "How fast time passes." Or, "We are passing the time in Chicago." Is time something which passes us like a stream, or is it something which we are passing in the stream of existence? We say, "There is no time like the present." But what is the present? We can't grasp it. The moment we try to put our finger on it, it is gone.

Well, let us not spend any more time exploring the meaning of time, but let us start with a desire which we all should share. It was expressed by Paul when he wrote to the Ephesians: "Look carefully then how you walk, not as unwise men but as wise, making the most of the time." We all admit that it is our God-given duty to make

130

the most of the time allotted to us. How can God help us to fulfill this duty?

First of all, God can help us to budget our time. The late President Faunce of Brown University once gave a chapel talk to his students on the interesting subject "The Pleasures of Economy." He pointed out that in games and sports, one source of pleasure is in the limitation imposed. In baseball, for example, the player is allowed only three strikes. If the batter were permitted to strike at the ball as long as he pleased, the game would become too dull for the players or the spectators.

In golf a player is allowed one little ball and one drive at a time. If he could keep on driving until he got a drive which satisfied him, nobody would care to play with him. In fact, some of us would never get off the first tee!

Similarly, life is a game which has to be played within the limits of time. Yonder is a man who is spending his time in sleep. If it is needed sleep after useful work or useful service, then he is knitting up "the ravell'd sleave of care." But if it is just the sleep of laziness because he has no interest sufficient to keep him awake, then he is wasting time, just blotting it out.

Or yonder is a person who spends time in a drunken stupor or plotting some evil deed. Such a man is not merely wasting time. He is unraveling the life achieved in the past. To do wrong is to drop the spool of life's continuing thread and thus undo what we have done.

When we spend time in a way that adds to the elements of life already achieved, we are not losing time. Rather we are storing up capital for the future. We are making our minutes count. To live right is to live so that yesterday, today, and tomorrow add up to something useful and purposeful.

Jesus of Nazareth was the supreme master of the art

131

of spending time. He never let time master *him*. He did not give the impression of dashing about Palestine trying to save time and keep to schedule. Yet he knew that his earthly working days were short. He said so. There was an air of urgency about him, but there was no feverish hurrying.

He had time to sit and talk with individuals along the way. He paused to play with little children. He took time off to spend whole days in prayer. But was it time off? Off from what? Ah, he was not keeping to a calendar. He was fulfilling a life. And if we are to fulfill our lives, we must live our days to the full, put our whole selves into the moments so that the moments can become the bits of eternal life.

Some time ago I was caught in a crowd pushing through the gates to catch a train. The guard cried, "Take your time." I recalled how Christopher Morley pictures Saint Peter at the "Pearly Gates" saying to the eager entrants, "Take your eternity." What is time? Someday we shall know.

❧❧❧❧❧❧❧❧❧❧❧❧

MAKING TIME

Time is elastic. Some days stretch out with seeming endlessness, others snap past in a flash. An hour spent in a hospital awaiting the outcome of an operation may seem an eternity, while to a pair of lovers an hour is gone before they know it.

Since time is so elastic, God can help us to make time

by crowding more experience into certain magic moments. By that I do not mean rushing around fussing with more things or trying to cram more thrills into a crowded schedule, as some tourists try to "do Rome" in an afternoon or try to take in a half-dozen night clubs before closing time.

We can compute man-hours of manual labor and the horse-power of machines, but who can say how much thought and feeling can be put into an hour? We can open our minds and hearts to a greater flow of thought and emotions. Recall how Handel composed "The Messiah." For twenty-three days he was completely withdrawn from the things of this world. He was so immersed in his music that the food brought to him was sometimes left untouched. Describing his feeling when the "Hallelujah Chorus" burst on his mind, Handel said, "I did think I did see all Heaven before me, and the great God Himself."

We ordinary mortals do not have the capacity of a Handel, but we can have our high moments when we feel that "one crowded hour of glorious life is worth an age without a name." If we hold our minds to the highest we know and open our hearts to the best we feel, God fills our minutes with magic content.

Another way to make time is to decide in advance what you most want to do. We can always make time for a thing if we desire it enough. We commonly say that when you want a thing done, go to the busy person. We mean that he handles his time efficiently. He knows how to put first things first.

Hence it is a good thing to start the morning by making a preview of the day. Decide on the "musts." Emergencies may arise to interrupt your schedule, but don't let them sidetrack you. It was said of Oliver Cromwell that he always gave the impression of "going somewhere." He knew his goals and he was on his way, leaving the world to marvel at his energy and achievement.

God helps us to make time by living concurrently in other lives. There is a good sense as well as a bad sense in which a man can live a double life. I think of a father whose son died young. That father once told me that he felt he must somehow carry on his work, and he does double duty, exerting almost superhuman efforts.

During the last war a young naval officer of my acquaintance saw a shipmate die when his destroyer was hit. The young lieutenant said to me: "When I think of my future, the most compelling thought which comes to me is that I must carry on what that lad wanted his country to do."

God helps us to make time by living in lives that will come after ours. We can experience what George Eliot prayed for:

> Oh, may I join the choir invisible
> Of those immortal dead who live again
> In minds made better by their presence.

We are not limited to our own little span of years. Some of us will go on living in our children and grandchildren. Some will be living fifty years from now in the careers of those boys and girls whom they are helping through college. Some will be living a hundred years hence in movements and causes which they have aided.

Would we make the most of our time as Paul bade us? Then let us improve each passing moment, but also remember that we can make added time by extending our lives into lives and causes which will be going on far beyond our years.

DO IT YOURSELF—CAN YOU?

Today with our new psychological aids we are turning with fresh zeal to the study of ourselves. Our grandfathers cleared the wilderness, opened the frontiers, built the roads. But now that the external world has been mapped, we are setting out to clear the jungle of the mind.

We realize that our mind power must catch up with our machine power or we shall destroy ourselves. Dorothy Thompson once wrote, "The new worlds to conquer are not horizontal, they are vertical. They are in men's minds."

Yes, to these inner worlds of the mind we are returning. And for their conquest may we lay down a prescription given several centuries ago by one who made a defective body dynamic enough to undergo incessant travel and unspeakable hardship; one who rose to such stature that his shadow fell across the whole Mediterranean world. I refer to the Apostle Paul, and to his formula for self-mastery, which was: "Work out your own salvation with fear and trembling; for God is at work in you, both to will and to work for his good pleasure."

Let us look at the first half of that formula: "Work out your own salvation." In this self-help we have our new psychological aids of which Paul never heard. We have learned about that region of the mind which lies below the level of conscious thought. We know that down there are our suppressed wishes, our lost memories, our instinctive drives, our sources of mysterious strength. We have discovered that this hidden dynamo of the unconscious can be made to work for us.

We have modern ways of talking ourselves into new states of mind. We were told some years ago by Dr. Coué that we could sweeten our dispositions and lighten our shadows by repeating to ourselves, "Day by day in every way, I am getting better and better." We know that our minds are most susceptible to these health-giving suggestions at certain times, as for instance in the morning before the waking censor has closed the mental shutters, or at night when approaching slumber evokes the mood of relaxation. We now recognize that our minds can be made to work for us even while we sleep and often untie the knotty problem which has baffled our waking hours.

With all these modern scientific insights, why call in God to help us? For one thing, the thought of God imparts a sense of sacred responsibility to the process of self-improvement. You work out your own salvation with fear and trembling, for as Paul says, "You are not your own; you were bought with a price."

This is not the craven cowardice of one who dreads future punishment, but the sensitive carefulness of one who handles entrusted funds with more care than his own. It is the feeling of a good son who fears that he may hurt his father. It is the feeling of a good father who fears he may let his family down.

Also, God keeps us from thinking too highly of ourselves. Everett King tells of a large trailer truck which got stuck beneath the overhead girders of an underpass in Oklahoma. The traffic was stalled. The highway experts worked for hours to release the truck. Power trucks tried to push or pull it free.

Finally a little boy, who was eagerly watching, asked this simple question, "Why don't you let the air out of the tires of the trailer?" The air was let out and the truck was released. Often a divine deflation of our pride will help us out from under our difficulties.

Furthermore, God lifts our spirits when we are feeling low. Listen to a man talking to himself. The man is Henri Amiel, professor in the Academy at Geneva. He has just visited his physician and learned that he has an incurable malady.

Next morning he writes in his Journal: "On waking it seemed to me that I was staring into the future with startled eyes. Is it to me that these things apply? Health cut off means marriage, travel, study, and work forbidden or endangered. It means life reduced in attractiveness and utility by five-sixths." But go on and hear the last words of Amiel's Journal entry, "Thy will be done." There he is talking to God.

When the doctor tells you the worst, can you talk yourself out of your depression? Not very well unless you have a God to talk to.

✠✠✠✠✠✠✠✠✠✠✠✠

DOING AND UNDOING

It is folly to torture our minds with regrets over what cannot be changed. We must master the art of leaving if we are to master the art of living.

One of the very important questions of successful living is when to go forward and forget and when to go back and remember.

Some parts of our past should be left for dead. We should learn how to close the gate on what should be forgotten, so that yesterday's pack of yelping worries do not keep hounding us to destroy today's peace of mind.

Most of us have a tendency to keep some things which should be left behind. When we move from one residence to another, we discover how many articles we have kept stored up which we shall probably never use but which we hate to throw away.

We preserve many customs which no longer serve any useful purpose. Dorothy Canfield Fisher has called attention to the buttons sewed on the outside seam of a man's coat sleeve back of the wrist. What are those buttons for? A century and more ago gentlemen wore white ruffles at their wrists, and they were buttoned snugly back to keep them from being soiled. The buttons are still put on coats long after their purpose has disappeared.

We need the courage to change what should be changed, the patience to endure what cannot be changed, and the wisdom to know the difference.

And wisdom should tell us that there is a difference between forgetting the evils done to us and the sins we ourselves commit. Suppose a reckless driver had run into my car last month. The damage is done. The incident is over. I should forget it. It does no good to keep thinking about it.

But if I were the reckless driver who caused the damage, then that recklessness is in my own nature. It remains with me unless I get rid of it. If I don't care enough about my carelessness to correct it, I add to the sinfulness of it. Hence, I must not try to bury my own wrongdoing in forgetfulness. If I do, I am likely to go on repeating the evil deeds. We cannot toss our sins aside and forget them, because in doing so we keep on sinning. The bad memories we thought were buried keep working below our conscious mind.

Moral failure cannot be healed easily. When a person has disobeyed his conscience, betrayed his ideals, tarnished his character, trespassed on others—these things do not lose their bad look when brought to light. They look worse instead of better. And the hope of cure lies in making them look so bad that the sinner turns from them in abhorrence and disgust.

It does not do any good just to remember sins which we cannot undo. To sit and brood over them, to keep asking, "Why did I do it?" to keep saying, "What a fool I've been!" to keep looking at the wreckage we have wrought by our misdeeds—all that is futile and gnawing remorse. It tortures the mind without cleansing the conscience. Like a rocking chair, remorse keeps us moving but doesn't get us anywhere.

Some years ago, during a final World Series game, a decisive contest, a well-known catcher failed to stop a ball. It bounded by him and the winning run scored. His teammates lost perhaps a thousand dollars each. This fine fellow brooded over the incident. It nearly ruined his career. The club manager talked with him.

"Forget it," he said.

"I can't forget it," replied the catcher. But he did forget it and went on the next year to greater glory.

❖❖❖❖❖❖❖❖❖❖❖❖

LOOSE ENDS

Let us suppose I own a sailboat. I do not possess one, but it is a pleasant thought to ponder. I go down to the shore to take it out for a sail. A sailor at the little harbor where it is kept comes up to me and says: "Your tackle hangs loose; it cannot hold the mast firm in its place or keep the sail spread out." I would at once look to the loose ends of my sailing equipment.

Centuries ago the prophet Isaiah looked at his nation and used those same words in the thirty-third chapter of his prophecy.

What does that statement mean when applied to a nation or a person? Well, I think it means that life needs tightening up if we are to be made shipshape.

Our lives have loose ends if our impulses are not organized. We are born little bundles of desire. The infant reaches out for anything that catches his fancy, and his fancy changes with almost every fleeting moment. If the child does not outgrow that impulsiveness, he remains childish. Some impulses must be curbed, others cultivated. Impulsive living leaves the heart empty.

I know a fellow who vowed he would not get "tied down" to any woman. He prided himself that he was footloose and fancy-free. His fancy was caught by almost every new girl he met. He frittered away his thirties in many passing flirtations and now, though far from poor financially, he is sort of a social tramp begging his morsels of satisfaction at the back doors of life.

A curious fact about life is that when we just let ourselves go and do what we like when we like it, we cease before long to like what we do. For this reason William James was wont to say a person should do one unpleasant duty every day just to keep himself in moral trim. If we never put ourselves out to curb some impulses, we eventually feel "put out."

In a hotel some time ago, I saw signs at various points reading, "For the convenience of our guests." Such suggestions are appreciated in a hotel. But a home hardly can be run as a convenience. Certainly, we want as many household conveniences as we can secure. But only when the members of the family share some uncongenial tasks and some mutual sacrifices do they come to enjoy the solid satisfactions and spiritual blessings of the home.

Likewise in our relationship with God we are a part of his family. And we cannot enter fully into the fellowship of God's family if we treat him and his church merely as a convenience. If we turn to God only when we feel the need of his help in trouble, we shall never know God's friendship. Or if we go to church only when we feel like it, or when we wish to use it for a marriage ceremony, we shall not receive the joy and peace and power of our religious faith. We must sometimes sacrifice our personal convenience and do some uncongenial tasks in the service of God and his other children.

A meeting was being held to promote a certain good "cause." A telegram was read from a man who liked to show his interest in good movements but never gave much thought or effort to them. In his message he said, "My heart is with you." When the chairman of the meeting read the wire, he added sarcastically, "We are glad to have Brother Jones's heart with us. We wish we had his head also."

We sometimes say, "I don't want to be tied down to any duties or commitments. I want to be free to choose what I wish to do when the time comes." I sympathize in part with that feeling. I do not like things to become so methodical that they are dull. But I raise the question with you whether in our desire to live the free life we may not be forgetting that one way to achieve freedom is to bring some actions under such automatic control that we do not have to spend time discussing them.

While we are so concerned to get ourselves in physical trim, let's get ourselves in moral trim by tightening up the loose ends of life.

BUILDING TO LAST

Look at the back of a dollar bill. Note the pyramid with the eye in the top. Now look at another picture. It is a picture of a tower rising until its top is lost in the clouds. I first saw it as a boy in an old family Bible. It was entitled "The Building of Babel."

The Bible verse which accompanied it voiced motives as modern as the last meeting of some Chamber of Commerce. The builders said, "Go to, let us build us a city and a tower, whose top may reach unto heaven; and let us make us a name, lest we be scattered abroad upon the face of the whole earth." (K.J.V.)

Those early builders of Babylon expressed a threefold desire. First of all, they wanted a city. Man is not content merely to have a home. He wants a home among other homes. When the curtain of recorded history first rises, man is seen living in groups, in tribes, or villages.

The Indians who inhabited America's great Southwest before the coming of Columbus had the vast open spaces. Nevertheless they piled their dwellings almost on top of one another, like our city apartments.

It was not the dearness of land but the dearness of life which drove them together. Men want to live in community, in fellowship with one another. They wanted that in ancient Babylon. They want it now.

Secondly, they said, "Let us build us . . . a tower, whose top may reach unto heaven." They were not content with homes just to shelter their bodies. Caves and huts would do that. But early man began to decorate his caves. Something in man craves beauty. He wants towers and monuments, paintings and symphonies.

Out of that urge have come the towers of Babylon, the haunting loveliness of the Taj Mahal, the stone tapestries

142

of the Alhambra. Man is a strange being! He feels a presence that disturbs him with the joy of elevated thoughts. His body may return to dust, but in his mind is "the stuff as dreams are made of."

With his hands he may be laying bricks in the Bronx. But with his mind he is building castles in Spain. Men want towers, beauty, what we call "the higher things of life." They wanted them in Babylon. They want them now.

Thirdly, the builders of Babel said, "Let us make us a name." We teach our children that they should make names for themselves. Do we not all like to be known by name?

Some years ago a lawyer was brought to New York from a small city in the Middle West to be an attorney for a great railroad. After a time in New York he walked into his office and announced that after the following January he would be found back in his home town. Back there, he said, the boys on the street called him by name when he went to work. He could not stand being lost in the crowds of the metropolis, nameless and unknown.

It is human nature to want the feeling of worth and dignity which comes from being known by name. Each of us wants to be somebody, to make a name for himself. They wanted it in ancient Babylon. We want it today.

But where are those towers of Babylon now? Excavators hunt for their ruins among centuries-old rubble.

Now look back at the pyramid on your dollar bill. There is a great eye at the apex. America believes that it takes a higher vision and power than man's to build our towers.

We want to live together in cities, but we have learned what the psalmist said: "Except the Lord build the house, they labour in vain that build it: except the Lord keep the city, the watchman waketh but in vain" (K.J.V.).

Man cannot lift himself to heaven by his own bootstraps. Two wars have shown us the collapse of human cleverness. We cannot live together in peace either at home or abroad unless we see our fellow men as God's children.

We have a common word that has come down to us from the old towers of Babel. It is the word "babble." We know what it means. A babble of voices is a mixture of unintelligible human words.

If we, like the ancient Babylonians, try to build without God, our conferences, our Congress, our United Nations become a babble.